To Suzanne,
Happy Hushpuppy
Eating!

EXPLODING
HUSHPUPPIES

MORE STORIES FROM HOME

Leslie Anne Tarabella

Leslie Anne Tarabella

WESTBOW
PRESS®
A DIVISION OF THOMAS NELSON
& ZONDERVAN

This book is a work of non-fiction. Unless otherwise noted, the author
and the publisher make no explicit guarantees as to the accuracy of
the information contained in this book and in some cases, names of
people and places have been altered to protect their privacy.

WestBow Press books may be ordered through booksellers or by contacting:

WestBow Press
A Division of Thomas Nelson & Zondervan
1663 Liberty Drive
Bloomington, IN 47403
www.westbowpress.com
844-714-3454

ISBN: 978-1-6642-0653-3 (sc)
ISBN: 978-1-6642-0654-0 (hc)
ISBN: 978-1-6642-0652-6 (e)

Library of Congress Control Number: 2020918627

Print information available on the last page.

WestBow Press rev. date: 10/07/2020

From "A Child's Garden of Verses" to tall tales around the table,
I dedicate this book to my first storytellers,
my mother Alma, and to the memory of my father, Cordell.

LET ME TELL YOU A STORY . . .

This place we call home looks different for everyone. A home full of screaming children brings joy to some and hair-pulling anxiety to others. A quiet home for one can bring happiness and a home for two in the mountains sounds dreamy — or like a deep nightmare, depending on who the other person is, of course! Just as none of us can find the perfect words to describe love, we can't begin to grasp all that home can mean.

My home is both modern and very old fashioned. We have a robotic lawnmower, voice-activated thermostats, automatic door locks and so many gadgets I can't even turn the lights on sometimes because I've forgotten the thing-a-ma-jig for how to control the doo-hickey. And yet, we've always sat down to a home-cooked meal at night and spent time talking with our two sons around the table. I bake birthday cakes from scratch and often cook with food I've grown in my garden. I don't quilt or churn butter, but I think it would be fun to learn — oh, who am I kidding? My Great-Granny Laird would tell me, "Honey, go buy yourself a blanket and some butter and spend the extra time at the beach!" I always did like that woman.

You'll see several stories in this collection that reflect my faith, because that's the rock on which our home is built. How something can be both ancient and freshly contemporary is a beautiful mystery, and yet my traditional faith in God is a present-day comfort. This living faith will never go out of style.

The readers of my newspaper column and blog have always been encouraging and seem to value their homes and families as much as I do, even when they are very different from mine. I love reading the feedback they send with stories about their own families. It's a small world where we find comfort through our memories that often bring both tears and laughter.

No matter where or how we may live, we're connected in this world, and sharing stories with one another helps us appreciate and celebrate life. Chaos, trouble and strife may swirl around us, like hot boiling hushpuppies popping through the air, but when the dust settles and we close our eyes at night, we should always feel safe and in love with this place we call home.

Thank you for reading,
Leslie Anne

CONTENTS

EXPLODING HUSHPUPPIES

Even though it's totally low class and unladylike, I cuss just a little bit — but only when triggered by a bad hushpuppy.

Like most Gulf Coast families, we started frying the fish and hushpuppies outside in a large deep fryer because it was too dangerous to heat all that oil indoors, plus your house smells like fish for a week afterwards.

Our family learned the hard way to move the event outdoors when we gathered at my grandparents' house in DeFuniak Springs and there were too many cooks in the kitchen who all decided to add a little bit of baking powder to the hushpuppy mix. One by one, each took a turn adding a pinch of this and a teaspoon of that to the bowl.

I was about eight years old and sat and watched as the ladies in the family prepared the fish dinner, caught earlier that day by the men.

As the balls of batter were dropped into the boiling pot of

oil on the stove, my mother, grandmother and aunts busied themselves with the baked beans, slaw, tea and fish. Then, all respectable lady like decorum broke loose and squeaky-clean Baptist chaos ruled the room.

The addition of extra baking powder made the hushpuppies explode and shoot through the kitchen. Lava-like lumps of batter were popping and flying everywhere, even sticking to Grandmother's 12-foot-tall ceiling.

Mass chaos ensued and screaming women bumped into each other as they tried to dodge the cornmeal- and-onion-laced inferno. Sizzling, screaming and sliding on the oil-slicked floor turned the kitchen into a hot mess.

Granny got the broom to knock the hushpuppies off the ceiling but realized they were still dripping with scalding oil. My aunt decided it would help if she took off her apron and waved it about her head like a wasp was in the room. Another woman grabbed the fly-flap, thinking she could swat the boiling balls of batter like Babe Ruth.

Never had I seen so many women unable to express themselves. A bunch of Baptists unpracticed in the art of proper cursing, they spewed out a string of nonsense. "Get the-the thingamajig — but Mama — hold on!" "Put the doohickey round — NO!" "Somebody get — duh-mo-no -Jell-O—hello - move — wait!" "The — oh, Lordy help us!" They sputtered and spewed and exploded as much as the hushpuppies. No one knew what to do nor did they know what to say.

The men ran into the room, making matters worse because they all wanted to take charge and tell everyone what to do, all while molten blobs of half-fried hushpuppies rained down on them like D-Day.

As I sat and watched, uncharacteristically calm from the safety of the far side of the kitchen table, I decided I would learn to cuss just a little bit when I grew up so as to be prepared to adequately express myself in times of an emergency. If you need to grab the attention of people in the room, a well-placed forbidden word can be a powerful tool.

In my family, a naughty word thrown into the conversation was downright shocking and cause for immediate attention if not a literal sudden death.

To confirm my suspicion about powerful forbidden words being useful at the right time and place, a little boy in Sunday School had pointed out some words in the Bible that got the attention of the grown-ups. A very hot place commonly spelled on the playground with "double hockey sticks" and an alternative word describing a donkey usually made the Sunday School teacher blush, fan herself and say, "I swanee!"

It was the only time I'd ever seen a Sunday School teacher take a Bible away from a child. "Close that book now!" she said. "Don't be using it for such things as that!" The kid pointed his finger to something in Exodus and said, "But it's right here in the Bible!"

If we'd had a good Episcopalian in the family who could have stood on a chair and screamed a few choice words to get everyone's attention, it could have saved a few trips to the emergency room. But the chaos continued until the last hushpuppy dripped from the ceiling. Grandmother's bold Presbyterian childhood took over and she exclaimed, "Mercy daisy!"

To this day, I can't tolerate a bad hushpuppy. If they are perfectly round, and dense, I know they've been frozen, and if they are bland, I have to push them aside. Just to keep in practice in case of an emergency, I whisper to my husband, "Somebody needs to get on the ball because this hushpuppy tastes like . . . and the poor man's face drains of color because I've shocked him once again with my expansive ladylike vocabulary. Forgive me and thank you, God, for the gift of a good hushpuppy.

THIS PASSIONATE PLACE WE CALL HOME

Earleena was telling the Committee for the Preservation of Loveliness about a flower in her yard that blooms only once a year. She wanted us to see it, but as with an expected baby, couldn't give us an exact day or time of the arrival. Dawna Dee, a local attorney, excitedly said she had seen a similar flower when she was only four years old and clearly remembered the details.

Although I wasn't interested in a shy once-a-year flower, I was mesmerized by the entire conversation, which was loaded with great passion. The ladies' eyes twinkled, and they scooted to the edge of their seats as they spoke with excitement. Normally reserved, they put their teacups down and punctuated their descriptions with wiggly fingers. As true Southern ladies, they began planning a flower-viewing party, complete with flower-shaped cookies, tiny sandwiches and an all-white dress code so the guests would match the flower.

People with passion are beautiful. Whether it's an elusive flower or a new hound dog, we are easily prone to bursts of enthusiasm. Repairing a record player that still plays our mama's vinyl albums or finally mastering the perfect hummingbird cake

— whatever excites a Southerner to the point of passion ignites contagious elation. Our faces light up, and there's a lilt in our voices when we discuss what we love.

Although people all over the world have passions and can be experts in certain fields, Southerners tend to express their passions in unique ways that often amaze others.

A variation of wearing our hearts on our sleeves, we feel the need to announce our passions on our chests. Favorite schools, trucks, bands, beverages and politics can all be found printed across our shirts. Some find our fervor for torso-billboards unusual and almost pushy. We find their solid black shirts boring and sad. We ring cowbells, fly flags, march in parades and enter the county fair — all to celebrate a few of our favorite things.

Other parts of the country are either bland, with not much passion at all, or have a different style of passion unique to their area, which can be downright alarming to those unfamiliar with the strong language and interesting hand gestures used to express their passions. (Just speaking from experience — "Mercy daisy. That's not what a car horn is for!")

We aren't passionate only about our jobs, hobbies and food, but also for the land itself and the people who live here. We'll work ourselves into a frenzy fighting to keep something the same, then the very next week wave signs on the street corner demanding change. We cry for the national anthem and laugh hysterically at old jokes then curse the referee, all within five minutes.

Our passions are based in love, which is what makes them so beautiful. We've been taught to love and trust each other from the time we were children. Shaking hands, looking someone in the eye, smiling and holding doors for people have taught us the basics of love. Is it any wonder that loving one another spills over to love for other things, like teaching children to read, saving kittens, collecting pocketknives or growing tomatoes?

We are interesting people because we notice and are passionate about the little things in life that make us happy. That's why we are passionate about this place we call home.

USE THE
GOOD CHINA

My brother and I were settled deep into the orange shag carpet watching *The Brady Bunch* when we heard an enormous crash. My mother, who had fortunately stepped into the garage for a moment, thought an airplane had landed on the roof. We rushed into the kitchen and found the long row of cabinets mounted above the sink had ripped loose from the wall and tipped forward, where they were stopped and held in mid-fall by the wall-mounted telephone.

The doors dangled open, and every single dish and glass we owned had been launched across the room, where the floor was covered with shards of china and glass about two inches deep.

Mother was in shock and sick that all her beautiful Haviland wedding china had been lost. Living on my dad's minister's salary, we didn't have a real china cabinet for the fine china, so it had all been stored with the everyday dishes in the kitchen cabinets. Every single piece of the old and the new — from elegant crystal to cheap glasses featuring the Hamburglar — had been smashed onto the tile floor.

For years, my mother was too practical to replace her dishes with anything fancy. She picked out a pretty everyday pattern we used for all occasions and supplemented the holiday season with the Nikko Christmas pattern. (No matter how down-to-earth they are, Southern ladies must have a Christmas pattern.)

Maybe "the big crash" is why I now love pretty dishes and use them every time we eat. Paper plates only appear as a palette for mixing paint or to drain fried foods. I've even been known to take the good stuff on picnics.

I have the fine china given to me as wedding gifts, the Lenox Holiday pattern, a vintage Liberty Blue set I've collected piece by piece from antique and thrift stores and even a bright yellow set I earned from shopping at Delchamps. Of course, there's the smattering of Blue Willow (which is what Aunt Bee used in Mayberry). I also have my husband's grandmother's set with little pink rosebuds I use at Easter. Anytime there's food served in my house, it's always placed atop a real plate.

Some think it's a chore to use their good dishes, but really, you just swish them off in the sink, and you're good to go. My china isn't super expensive, but all of it evokes special memories.

Each day you don't have your wedding gifts pulverized on the kitchen floor is reason to celebrate. Every day you live to eat another meal, even if it's only buttered toast, is a reason to go to the effort to use a pretty plate.

A seashell on the bookshelf, a wildflower in a Co-cola bottle next to the bed, our children's artwork displayed in a frame or a pretty plate for our food — all show appreciation for the gifts of simple beauty.

We shouldn't have to wait until Christmas to pull out the good china. If a plate occasionally crashes to the floor, we should learn to shout, "Whoopee!" because it's the sound of a life being enjoyed and well lived. Of course, if it's the sound of your entire cabinet crashing, it's okay to just sit and cry. But then, there are new collections to discover.

WHY THE CARS STAND STILL FOR A FUNERAL

A friend new to our area was a few minutes late to lunch and told us how she was stuck in traffic that had stopped for a funeral procession. She asked if this was a local law or just another Southern quirk she didn't understand.

"Both," said Trudy." "It's a quirk we consider to be law." Rhonda added "We kind of make up our own laws around here if you haven't noticed." The lunching ladies tried to explain the custom but found it difficult to put into words exactly why we pull over for those headed to their final resting place. It's kind of like trying to explain why we give our children four names and use every one of them when we stand on the porch and call them. It's just what we do. And you don't want to encounter the scowling faces of other drivers as you zip past the procession. No matter how old you are, your mother will hear about it by the end of the day.

When someone you love dies, your whole world stops. You think nothing will ever be the same and find it difficult to see other people still going about their everyday lives. Your heart seems to stop, your smile fades and it's hard to even draw a breath without actual physical pain. When strangers stop their cars, and allow you to pass, it wraps one of the saddest days of your life in kindness. You know others are acknowledging your grief and feel like they are reaching out to give your hand a squeeze. It's common decency at its finest.

I'm sure the tradition of pulling over began in small towns where most people knew each other. When a funeral procession passed by, even if they didn't know the deceased well enough to attend the funeral, they at least knew some of the kinfolk and understood their pain.

Neighbors around here share tools, garden vegetables, recipes and faith. To share suffering is part of the package of living in a tight community. As our cities have grown and new friends from outside have joined, it's difficult to explain why it's so important to share grief. We embody the old saying, "Joy shared is multiplied and grief shared is divided."

From the point of traffic control, it also makes sense to pull over, so the mourners can stay together and avoid being lost on a side road.

On a cold January day, our family made their way to Cedar Creek Cemetery in Hartselle to bury my grandmother. Vehicles slowed to a stop, and some men even got out of their cars, and placed their hats over their hearts. Did they know Grandmother? Did they know our family? Maybe — or maybe not, but the point was, they knew our sorrow. They knew someone in their community was gone and a family was forever changed.

I've always loved the story about my Florida grandparents, who once left town on vacation, and as they returned to their small town of DeFuniak Springs a few weeks later, passed by the cemetery, where they observed a funeral in progress. Grandmother explained, "We stopped, because we figured we'd know who the funeral was for, and sure enough, it was one of our friends who had died while we were gone." They knew their community well enough to know the connections reached far and deep and would, of course, envelop them.

When we pause our busy day and put our plans on hold for even a brief moment to honor a family in our community, we think about how we're all attached in some way. Maybe this is the family who owns the local store where we shop, or perhaps it's the family of the man who drives your children to school on his bus. Speaking to each other in public enables us to know one another. We're friendly in life, so we're loyal in death.

Sitting on the side of the road and observing car after car driving by with their lights shining bright, and passengers dabbing their eyes and hanging their heads low, hurts us all. Our town has changed again, but life moves on while the cars stand still.

WHEN PARENTS BREAK A PROMISE

Pinky swears, whispers of secret club loyalties, no-girls-he-man-women-hater clubs like Spanky and Alfalfa had, all taught us to keep our childhood promises no matter what. So when parents change their minds, children tend to flip out and try to guilt them into following the unspoken rule of never-ever-ever going back on their word. "But a promise is a promise," they literally cry.

What the children and teenagers don't realize, and actually many adults forget, is that parents have a free pass to change our minds anytime we want. Sure, it isn't good to flip-flop and be wishy-washy, or else the kiddies won't be able to trust us. Our word should be good, but every now and then, when necessary, we should be flexible and bold enough to tell our offspring we've been wrong and need to stop and rethink our original decision.

My elder son is musically gifted but hated band, because in all honesty, he was too lazy to practice his trumpet. The easy way out was to moan and groan and beg me to let him quit. He was such a pain in the neck, I told him he could quit before high school started. Oh — joy! His demeanor changed, and he started thinking about other groups to join.

But then . . . I had a mom moment and realized he wouldn't join other groups. Although he had attended baseball camps and had proven he could throw a baseball with great force and hit a tiny target, he wanted no part of it. He could sketch and draw beautifully but didn't want to join the art club. Recognizing that every teen needs to find a sense of belonging, especially in a large school, I knew he needed a clan — a team. Knowing how fun high-school band was for me, I knew if he only gave it a try, he'd love it.

But I had promised he could quit. Oh, dear. I knew he'd pitch a fit. And he did.

Tears. Stomping of the feet. His loud squeaking preadolescent voice slinging arrows and spears at me. "But you promised I could quit!" I tried to calmly explain how I knew I had promised, but after thinking about it, decided this time I needed to go back on my word and try another plan. We rearranged our agreement and decided that if he tried band during his freshman year and didn't like it, then he could absolutely quit, with no opposition from me. I think I also had to throw in a new pair of sneakers.

Summer band camp rolled around a week before the start of classes, during the hottest time of the year in humid South Alabama. Gathering his despised trumpet and a giant thermos of ice water, he mumbled as he headed off to the all-day camp. That night, a friend dropped our trumpeter off at the door, and in teenage style, he dramatically collapsed on the floor in the middle of the family room.

"How did you like it?" we held our breath and asked.

With barely enough energy to lift his head, he said, "It was awesome."

"How did you like the director, Mr. Duncan?"

"He's awesome," was the weak but truthful reply.

Harrison loved band and found his tribe in the brass section.

He also found some cute friends in the flag corps, and his musical abilities soared. And in some strange twist of ironic fate, he became the drum major his senior year, which led to huge boosts in self-confidence, college scholarships and also the perfect excuse to finally ditch the trumpet, which was his evil plan all along. No lie, at his senior symphonic concert, he surprised us by happily playing the triangle.

When we know what is best for our children means going back on our word, we need to remember, as the rule makers, parents also have the right to be the rule changers. And if done in love, and in a wise way, it will all work out — and no one will have to play the trumpet forever.

WITNESS PROTECTION

I heard a rumor that the Witness Protection program doesn't relocate people to the South very often, because when you're in hiding, the last place you want to be is where everyone asks you a million questions.

I never realized our inquisitive nature was unusual until new acquaintances from the Midwest told me they couldn't get their yard work done here because of all the people who wanted to talk to them.

"Where are you from?" "How long have you lived here?" "Do you have people here? Because I swanee, you look just like one of the Hilderguards who were raised down in the valley."

If you want to hide out, then the Southern states are not the place for you.

Good-mannered mamas taught us we'd be considered backwoods clods if we didn't visit the new neighbors and properly welcome them. "I baked these brownies for you and included our phone number just in case you ever need anything." Followed up with, "And do you mind if I have your number? I noticed yesterday that you didn't bring your garbage can back from the road until late afternoon, so I was concerned you might be down with a cold and need some soup."

"Is there a Mrs. Jones inside? I haven't seen anyone with you when you come and go and would love for you to meet my niece if you're available. She can cook up a storm and won the Miss Strawberry Festival Queen title in 2008 — do you want her phone number?"

New residents to our area said they've learned not to be offended when strangers start talking to them. Standing in lines, walking through the parking lot, picking up some chicken for supper, everyone wants to say hello and has questions about something or the other. "Where did you get those shoes? They are absolutely darling!" "My brother has that same car and loves it. Do you like yours?" Even brief comments ultimately lead to longer conversations. "Blue looks good on you." "Where do you get your hair cut? It's so sassy!" "Are you Darleen and Bill's girl?"

Then, of course, we have to discuss the weather with our new and old friends. Hot, cold, humid, windy — we feel compelled to make comments on the obvious, and even though it's mundane, something good always results from our ramblings. "My neighbor's air conditioning went out and, poor thing, she's about to bake to death." "You mean Miss Ruby Nell on the corner of Oak and 17th?" "Yes, she's had her windows open for two days now waiting on the repairman." "Well, the Presbyterian church is giving out box fans. I can carry one by her place later today."

I guess that's the reason Southerners are such a chatty society. While social media spreads basic information, the computer offers no real connection for hearing the fear, hope, sadness or joy in each other's voices. Emojis don't do justice when it comes to seeing the real glimmer of a grin or twinkling in an eye.

Vacation photos look perfect on the screen, but when we run into our friend in the drugstore buying four bottles of calamine lotion, we understand the week in the mountains wasn't so perfect after all, and their outbreak of poison ivy may call for some hydrangeas from the yard — tied with a blue ribbon — and a batch of Granny's poultice.

What we do best is connect with each other, and striking up conversations with newcomers is our way of drawing them into our world and learning about how we can love them as one of our own. We cherish our relationships, even if it's only casually knowing a person by face from the coffee shop. We talk to learn, and we learn because we care. We must understand you before we can love you.

Keeping to yourself in the South is difficult. Avoiding conversations with the locals can lead to loneliness, no hydrangeas when you're itchy, no fan on a hot day and no phone number for the 2008 Strawberry Queen. And who really wants to live like that?

A JOB TO MAKE
YOU SMILE

I was visiting a large museum, and although it was filled with gorgeous art, it also contained one of my least favorite things — shoving rude tourists. I approached the bored security guard, who immediately sized me up as a middle-aged woman and automatically pointed towards the ladies' room. Instead of following his directions, I used my terrible French, and thinking about the crowd, asked if he ever had the chance to be alone in the room.

Surprised by my question, the man in his early 30s took a moment, slowly grinned and said in equally terrible English, "Yes, sometimes I arrive early in the morning and stand with self — alone with her." He pointed to a spot in front of the Mona Lisa while he took another deep breath. "It is the favorite — good — best part of my job."

The "favorite, good, best" part of a job is what we all want to find. Daily drudgery, endless boredom and low pay can somehow all be worth it if there is a moment of glory when everything comes together and we can say, "Ah . . . this is why I do this every day."

A young mother drags through hour after hour of reading books, wiping sticky fingerprints off the furniture and changing diapers only to have a chubby face press a warm kiss on her cheek by the glow of a Thomas the Tank Engine nightlight. That's when she feels like she's alone with a masterpiece.

After working tirelessly for months, the brick mason walks by a year later with his father and swells with pride when he's told what a good job he's done. "Almost as good as my work when I was your age," his dad laughs, which makes his son forget the long hot days of work and instead bask in the glow of his dad's approval.

Clearing an innocent person of a crime, managing a store, operating heavy equipment or performing music, every single job should have a moment that makes us feel like we're releasing goodness into the world.

If you love the thought of educating children, you often become a teacher, but those who cook in the hot lunchroom or clean the classrooms or answer the office phones are also contributing to the overall growth of little minds. So yes, there really is a beautiful purpose in those delicious-smelling rolls in the cafeteria, and love and encouragement can be reflected in the shiny floors.

For a bundle of different reasons, robots will soon replace many workers, yet it's almost certain that those who approach their job with a positive attitude will land in another, perhaps even better position. A person's good character will propel them into careers where work and satisfaction intertwine.

When we discover true joy in our work, we've connected our souls to something greater than a mundane chore. Paychecks and awards don't compare to the purpose we find when our hearts are in the right place. The stressed-out security guard knows if he can put up with irritating tourists a little longer, he'll eventually be able to stare into the eyes of a masterpiece and return the most famous smile in the world. He's found the secret to turning a long, exhausting day into the "favorite, good, best" job ever.

WHAT WILL YOU DO WITH 940 SATURDAYS?

Poor Opie. He had to miss football practice to take piano lessons from Miss Clara and he hated them. But after just a few lessons, Opie learned he had an ear for music and started playing guitar in a groovy rock and roll band. Well . . . perhaps I'm scrunching two episodes together, or maybe it's *The Brady Bunch* I'm thinking of. But no matter, we've all seen the story on TV and in real life where a child was coerced, forced, bribed or tricked into doing something they didn't want to do, then suddenly realized it was something amazing.

I fear the days of rearing a child "buffet style" have come and gone. No longer do parents insist their children try a little bit of everything, but instead, have them focus on one main dish. Sure, your kid loves soccer, but how do you know they won't love making pottery or camping or dancing if they are busy with soccer 24 hours a day? If they try an activity once and don't like it, parents are tempted to throw their hands in the air and say, "I tried, but he just hates the clarinet, so I'm not going to make him do it anymore." But Mr. and Mrs. Fountain should insist little Pete keep trying, and even though they must endure the most agonizing sound known to man — a beginning clarinet player — the budding musical genius may eventually realize he loves it and wants to spend his life ruling the jazz scene in New Orleans.

Dr. Harley Rotbart has authored an article that reminds us we have approximately 940 Saturdays to spend with our children before they leave home. The article was supposed to motivate parents to spend more quality time with their children, yet I took it to mean we only have 940 Saturdays to expose our children to a world of options, variety, adventure and all the possibilities of our amazing world.

Children who are exposed to a wide range of experiences learn perseverance. They are therefore more likely to keep trying to master unfamiliar and new tasks in school like reading or focusing on what seems to be a boring teacher because she doesn't have a glowing, blinking screen attached to her forehead. Unfamiliar experiences teach adaptation, concentration and creativity.

"Children's theatre? Oh, Lula would never get onstage." But how do you know until you get little Lula to give it a try? She may be shy at first, but with encouragement could turn out to be the star in the Possum Playhouse all-child version of *Steel Magnolias*. "Her dress looked like she had two pigs a-fightin' under a blanket" (followed by wild applause, curtsies and blowing kisses).

A balanced diet of sports, music, art, science, dance, literature, theatre and travel make for a well-rounded child who won't grow up to bore their date by only being able to talk about one thing. And we can't forget the powerful potential of wide-open days with no plans at all, and no adults butting in, which often leads to the greatest childhood inventiveness ever.

Opie's childhood combination of football, music, tree climbing and fishing led him to a successful career directing award-winning films for the Mayberry Film Festival. Aunt Bee and Andy arranged his 940 Saturdays just right.

STEPPING OUT IN FAITH

Still preschool age and not fully able to understand the implications of seeing a man walk on the moon, I remember more about the overjoyed adults in the room than the actual lunar event. My parents, only in their late 20s, and my uncle who was visiting gathered around our small staticky TV set and cheered as Neil Armstrong stepped onto the moon. Later, as I played on my swing set, they handed me the newspaper and snapped my photo with the bold headline "America's Greatest Venture, Americans Walk on Moon." I grew up thinking space travel was normal.

When I was in college, the space shuttle Challenger exploded, and some classmates on our Tallahassee campus claimed to have seen the glaring streak in the sky. Even without social media, the news instantly spread across campus. As an aspiring teacher, I was devastated because I had cheered for educator Christa McAuliffe; losing her broke my heart.

In 2003, my son's first-grade class studied space and gathered in the lunchroom to watch the launch of the Columbia. The following Saturday, as we left for a soccer game, the news broke that upon atmospheric entry, Columbia had exploded and all aboard were lost.

My son sat in church the next day with his legs dangling off the pew, clutching his small space shuttle toy. He had brought it in his pocket and sat with his head hung low, not playing with it, but just gently holding it in hands that still had a chubby baby look to them.

For many years, we received email alerts so we could take our boys outside at night and watch the International Space Station glide overhead. In the stillness, we'd watch the stars twinkle and wonder aloud what the crew was doing.

An ordained elder in his Presbyterian church, Buzz Aldrin took the elements with him to observe communion in space. Before the lunar module hatch of Apollo 11 opened for the giant leap for mankind, Aldrin silently read John 15:5 and took the bread and wine to remember another sacrifice that made the impossible possible.

Aldrin later said he regretted releasing the information about his private communion experience because his desire was to represent all people of earth. Later, in 1969, when most faiths in America weren't as mainstream as Christianity, he explained, "At the time, I could think of no better way to acknowledge the Apollo 11 experience than by giving thanks to God."

No matter what our beliefs may be, I think we can agree that greater love hath no man than this: to step out into the dark unknown and be willing to risk everything for the future of little girls on their swing sets and little boys clutching their toys in church. It's for lunchrooms full of excited children and teachers who want to travel past the stars to show their students that dreams can come true. Blasting off into another world demonstrates great love for college students who stop and gasp in disbelief at bad news. It's bringing beautiful deep hope to people in faraway places and giving unity to all those who gaze up at "la bella luna" from every remote corner of the world. Risking one's life for medical, technological and scientific advancements all over the world is a selfless act based in love for all humankind.

THE HAIRCUT
OF BRAVERY

Like most Southern ladies, I place a great deal of importance on the appearance of my hair. It's our crowning glory and the actual place where we snuggle our real crowns and tiaras, so we take great care in making it as big, poufy, smooth, straight, sleek, flippy and curled as possible — depending on the trend of the moment and the humidity levels, of course.

That's why I surprised myself, my husband and everyone else when, one afternoon this past August, I stood in the kitchen and asked my husband to cut my hair off.

Just like that: "If I give you the scissors, will you cut three inches off my hair?"

Bob said, "Sure." He took the scissors and cut five inches off (oops), carefully placing each bundle of hair on the kitchen counter. The man knows no fear.

I wasn't taking any medications, nor was I tipsy or suffering from a head injury. I hadn't been bitten by a spider or baked too long in the sun. I don't know what in the tarnation got into me. I just wanted my hair cut right then and there, and I knew Bob was good for a spontaneous challenge.

There wasn't any big drama before or afterwards, I just called my "girl" at Bee-Bee's Beauty Barn the next morning and made an appointment for her to even up a few spots. She was kind and said she'd heard crazier stories about women nuttier than a fruitcake who whacked their hair off in the middle of a party or even moments before their wedding (who's crazy now?). She was impressed by my calmness, and I just slid back in the big spinning chair and let her finish the job.

Southern ladies rarely keep the same hairstyle very long. Our beauticians stay booked, and whether our 'dos are short and sassy or long and sleek, we purchase more appliances, accessories, styling gels, sprays, goop and glistening serums than people in any other place on the planet.

Short and better . . . for now.

I usually wear my hair long but have finally recognized a pattern of chopping my hair off every seven to eight years. It has little to do with the changing styles but instead reflects my changing life. If I can't control my children, husband, dog, parents, politics or terrorists, I can always control my hair (minus the humid days). All women are busy, but Southern ladies are taught to look pulled together in the midst of the storm. We were taught to hold our stuff together while everything else around us goes crazy. "Quit that blubbering and put on some lipstick," our mamas whispered.

To us, looking good isn't vanity, it's dignity. And if Southern women are anything, we are a dignified and determined bunch. You can burn our houses, steal our horses and destroy our crops, but we'll rip the curtains down and make a ballgown that matches the color of our eyes just to see you sweat. And our hair will look fabulous while we do it.

My husband did just what I asked — for once — and the new hairdo looked just like I envisioned. I gained a much-needed rush of control, trust and bravery all rolled into one haircut, and the price was just right.

THE HEALING POWER OF THE GULF

I spent my birthday writing the eulogy for my father's funeral. The same day I dropped my younger son off at college, Daddy went into the hospital and died less than a week later. I erroneously thought things couldn't get worse, but then a few days later a friend I had so much fun teaching Vacation Bible School with this past summer died unexpectedly, and just after Daddy's funeral, tragedy struck friends whose 24-year-old son was killed in a car accident.

My already bruised heart went into overload. I was exhausted but couldn't sleep and grieving but couldn't cry. My prayer was simply, "Help! I don't know what to pray for."

One dear friend, who is almost 100 years old, sent me a note to say that not a day has gone by since she lost her father that she hasn't seen his face or heard his voice. I didn't quite understand how that could happen.

Instead of lifting our eyes unto the mountains for our strength, our family has always felt power come from the blue-green waters at the beach, so as an act of distraction, my husband drove me down to the Gulf. Daddy loved to fish and would joke, "The Gulf is good for what ails you." Chiggers? Burn? Coughing? Sneezing? "Go jump in the salt water."

I dove into the waves with my broken heart and swam through the surf. The water was cool and shimmered in the early September afternoon. I picked up a few seashells and walked along the edge of the water.

Since Daddy served as the minister of music and youth director for several churches, we incorporated hymns into his funeral service. Mother was firm about keeping the tone uplifting, so even though I remembered Daddy saying he liked "The Old Rugged Cross," we decided to omit it in favor of more upbeat favorites like "Blessed Assurance." My dad's former youth choir members, who are now grown, made up a choir that sang the 23rd Psalm, and the two pastors who conducted the service were also former members of his youth group.

Returning from the beach, we decided to stop at a beachside joint and grab a bite to eat. While waiting on our food, a man entertained the crowd with his guitar. After singing several standard beach tunes, of all things, he began to sing "The Old Rugged Cross." Right there, in a restaurant with sand on the floor and a bar serving frozen margaritas as the stage's backdrop, was one of my dad's favorite hymns. Only in the South — the sunburned beach crowd quieted, and many began to sing along. With warm harmony drifting over the slaw and grilled oysters, tired children, still sticky with sunscreen, were cuddled in their mothers' arms, and the familiar hymn was never more perfect.

"Then he'll call me someday to my home far away, where his glory forever I'll share."

With my hair in ringlets still dripping with salt water and salty tears in my eyes, I suddenly remembered my friend's note. "There isn't a day that goes by when I don't see his face or hear his

29

voice." I finally understood that memories can surface when you least expect them, even in the sound of strangers singing together at a beachside dive. It was at that moment I heard him whisper, "I told you the Gulf is good for what ails you."

THE RECIPE FOR
MAKING A MAN

Snakes and snails and puppy dog tails. That's what he was supposed to be made of, and at first, I guess he was. Buzz Lightyear, bicycles and tuna fish sandwiches were the other parts. But now that he's graduating from high school and taking off into the world, I've realized there are many more components to my younger son than just slithery things and speckled pups.

This kid, who made an A in honors physics but can't figure out how to hang up a towel, is made from a combination of Eddie Van Halen, Casey Neistat and Jerry Seinfeld. There's a big helping of Steven Spielberg that forms the creative base of my budding filmmaker, with a dash of Picasso added for extra spice.

You can also find a large helping of America-loving Superman in my son, but if I'm being honest, there's also a sprinkling of Lex Luther — but who isn't a little bit of an evil genius at 18?

To balance the questionable influences, there have also been Sunday School teachers and Scout leaders who heaped on lessons of kindness and helpfulness. Even our pastor's mannerisms were reflected when Joseph gave his Eagle Scout speech. Starting with a corny joke, then without the use of notes and moving to the center aisle without a podium, he took off like lightning and wove a story that held us hanging on his every word. Although my own daddy has been a godly influence on my son, he also encouraged me to let Joseph just "be a boy" and secretly slipped him an endless supply of firecrackers, pocketknives and other forbidden treasures.

The only kid to ever foul out of an Upward Christian Basketball game, my Joe has a competitive spirit like John McEnroe's, but in an instant, can turn around to compliment a teammate or rival as if he were Tim Tebow.

Holding the hand of a friend who was dying much too young, and holding the hand of his sick granddaddy, Joseph has shown compassion far beyond his years. As early as the second grade, Joseph cried because he realized another boy had only one pair of uniform shorts, which were dirty and full of holes. Instead of making fun of him or seeking advice, my son already had a plan of action. "Let's buy him some new shorts and give them to the lady with the puppets (the guidance counselor) for her to give him so he won't be embarrassed." This part of Joseph is a full measure of Jesus himself that makes my heart happy.

Reading about Presidents Theodore Roosevelt and Ronald Reagan taught Joseph common sense and an appreciation of the great outdoors. I've often said if I'm ever lost in the forest, this child will be the one who rescues me. Because he's run his own successful business since he read Donald Trump's *The Art of the Deal* when he was only 16 years old, I've seen my son outwork and out-talent seasoned adult professionals, teaching him that hard work pays off.

If Joseph sat between Tom Sawyer and Huckleberry Finn at dinner, it would be difficult to tell the three apart, and like Aunt Polly, I also think, "There are some that believe he will be President yet — if he escapes hanging." Now that I think about it, that quote also fits my husband, who has been the largest influence on Joseph, which has always been my prayer.

Joe's played sports, musical instruments and pranks. He's loved dogs, curly-headed girls and sushi. He's learned technology, auto mechanics, foreign languages and how to scramble a great egg. He has a smile that will pierce your soul and will certainly slay me when I leave him at college this fall.

Over the next few years, the basic ingredients and traits gathered from others will meld together and cook to perfection to form a unique, confident man who is unlike anyone else. The adult form of Joseph will be unstoppable, but as his mom, beneath all the complicated layers, I'll always be able to see the original ingredients of snakes and snails and puppy dog tails.

TINY HOUSES AREN'T FOR SOUTHERNERS

I finally got a tour of a real-life tiny house, and after I squeezed my way past the combination kitchen table/bed, I understood why tiny houses aren't for Southern girls.

To prove my point, I heard about Mandy Mae, from Peachtree City, Georgia, who was engaged to be married to Tom from Bangor, Maine. Idealistic and adventurous, they thought it would be swell to live in a tiny house. Once called a "toolshed" or "playhouse" by most people, the miniature dwellings have been popularized by the HGTV television show *Tiny House.* This show features people who give up all the essentials of life, like sideboards, pianos and china cabinets to live in a sparsely appointed home no bigger than a bread box. The boxlike houses appeal to the free-spirited type, and Mandy Mae thought her giant love for Tom would compensate for the itty-bitty house.

"We'll be able to live anywhere," reasoned Tom, who began to grow a beard because his tiny house wasn't going to have room for both shaving cream and a razor.

"Isn't that just the definition of a camper?" his girlfriend wondered. Having been raised in a traditional Southern home with a front porch larger than three tiny houses, Mandy Mae (whose mother still called her Amanda Mabel) fretted about where she would store her Phi Mu scrapbooks, cedar chest, Grandad's Underwood typewriter and her mama's Pyrex casserole dishes. "Where will we keep the punchbowl?" she inquired.

"Punchbowl?" bellowed Tom. "We could drill a hole in the bottom and use it for a sink."

"What about Grandpa's manger scene he carved from the magnolia destroyed in Hurricane Camille, my childhood Easter baskets and the church cookbooks?" A sinister gurgle emerged from Tom, and at that precise moment, Mandy Mae realized that perhaps Tom wasn't her dream man after all.

Gifted at marriage with family crocheted tablecloths, deviled-egg plates and handmade dolls, every Southern bride knows how to make room for family treasures, even in the smallest apartment, but tiny houses make it impossible.

We aren't materialistic to the point of owning needless things; in fact, Southerners are very practical. It's just that we've been taught to appreciate all the bells and whistles that create memories and traditions. Napkins embroidered with the family monogram, Christmas ornaments, the family Bible and the old rug Great-Aunt Daisy carried back from Istanbul with a long-forgotten beau during her bohemian days — we have to make room for it all. It's our story.

While thinking the tiny house was a dorm room minus the "hang in there" kitty-cat poster, Mandy Mae overheard three words that finalized her decision: "low-flush toilet."

"That's when I called off the wedding," said the sensible young lady. "We realized we wanted different things in life — like a kitchen." The Georgia belle was comforted to realize that now she could inherit her grandparents' metal gliders for a proper screened porch.

Southerners have always reflected God's handiwork by being creators. Plowing, growing, building, sewing, hunting and cooking, we made things to survive and, somewhere along the way, saw the beauty in our work. The fact we appreciate and cherish good craftsmanship and family connections is no surprise, but we need a place to store it all. And unfortunately, it just won't fit into a tiny house. But for those who love the little homes, bless their tiny sweet hearts. We'll be glad to hold the family treasures for them.

WE CHEER
FOR COKE

Needing to keep my two boys productive and out of my hair when they were young, I came upon the idea of a job jar, seeded with a few little treats to sweeten the pot and make it more like a game.

I typed up, then cut and folded little strips of paper listing chores like: sweep the front porch, dust the baseboards, brush the dogs or scrub the toilet. Mixed in with the not-so-glamorous tasks, I showed the boys the coveted prize of "drink a Coke" — which in our house was a big treat since we only kept a few of the small cute bottles in the refrigerator for company.

"Play checkers with your brother," "build a blanket fort," "read a book in the treehouse" and "ride your bike" were also enticing rewards in the jar, but hands down, the chance of drinking a Coca-Cola was by far the top prize.

The rule was that no matter what chore you drew out of the jar, you had to do it, or else you'd lose your turn the next time. Therefore, the coveted Coca-Cola might go to your brother and you'd have to watch him drink it, which was a sure form of torture. Like addictive gamblers, the boys would hover over the jar, rubbing their little hands together and chanting, "Come on, drink a Coke — come on, drink a Coke!" Each wished with all their might for the cold bubbly drink to be theirs.

Although we are trying to cut back on sugar, Southerners are still loyal to the fizzy caramel-colored drink that gushes from the heart of Dixie. Nothing goes better with hotdogs or pizza, and good cooks know the secret ingredient of many dishes, like baked Easter ham or BBQ sauce, is often a can of Coke.

My great-uncle traveled to Atlanta soon after Coca-Cola was available. Returning home to the farm around Kinston, he tried to describe it to his 10 brothers and two sisters. "It tasted like your foot was asleep" was his perfect description of the tingly carbonated beverage.

After sweeping her house in DeFuniak Springs with such fury that the varnish nearly came off the floors, my grandmother would take a break. I'd follow her out to the front porch, where we'd sway back and forth in the blue metal glider and sip cold Co-Colas in glass bottles. I only remember her putting peanuts in our bottled Cokes once. She'd usually pour the fizzy drink into glasses filled with sharp squared-off ice cubes pried out of a metal ice-cube tray.

We drank Cokes in college to give us a caffeine boost for studying all night, but kids today think coffee works better. Oddly enough, I first learned to drink coffee by sipping the short-lived Coke Black, produced between 2006 and 2008, which was a bottled combination of Coca-Cola and coffee.

"What kind of Cokes do you want me to bring to the party?" was a legitimate question our mothers would ask their friends, and no one was confused.

"Why don't you bring a root beer and an orange? Verna Jean is bringing clear (Sprite)." Never at any time would anyone we know ask for a "soda" or a "pop," and a "soda pop" was just plain-out as weird as asking Grandpa if he wanted a falafel with a side of tahini.

Along with football allegiances, another great dividing line in the South is that some folks from North Carolina are loyal to Pepsi and consider it to be the official fizzy drink of the South, but where I come from, we are Coke people. "I'm sorry, we only have Pepsi" always elicited an audible groan from everyone at our table, and the poor waitress knew to just bring us tea instead.

Toning down the sweets these days is good, but when it comes to motivating little boys, you do what you have to do, and around my house, that always meant letting them cheer for a Coke.

SMART BOYS ARE THE BEST MYSTERY DATE

I never told a soul, but I always loved landing on the "nerd" when I played Mystery Date. I didn't have my own version of the popular Milton Bradley board game, but my friend always brought her big sister's game to slumber parties, where we'd take turns opening a plastic door to see who was picking us up for our pretend date.

We quickly realized the amount of pressure you put on the little doorknob would determine which young man was waiting on the other side, so we all tried our best to rig it so we'd land on the handsome young man wearing a white dinner jacket and holding a corsage — dreamy.

If I opened the door and found the preppy guy with a picnic basket, I thought he looked okay, but for some reason, he didn't strike me as trustworthy. The football player was popular with everyone, but I was convinced he'd only want to talk about sports because I'd heard about guys with one-track minds. The boy holding snow skis just confused us, because as little Southern girls, we didn't even know what snow was.

But the truth is, whenever I opened the door and found the "dud," as the game referred to him, I was completely smitten. With thick glasses and rumpled hair, he looked like today's hipsters who sit around coffee shops, so maybe I was ahead of the trend.

The sad thing is, when Mr. Dud showed up at the door, everyone would squeal and laugh. If I was the one who found him, I'd act mortified, but deep down inside, I felt something for the guy. He looked soulful and smart. He looked like he could whip that pen out of his shirt pocket and design a nuclear submarine, a symphony or a love letter.

To me, Dud-Dude was a thinker, and even though I was young, I already knew I loved brainy boys.

Smart guys are multifaceted and well rounded. They're the ones who can make a girl laugh by using wit, not foolish antics. They're the ones who lead the group, not by coolness or intimidation, but by being decisive and quick thinking.

Sure enough, when I met my husband, I didn't really think he was a dud, because he was as cute as the preppy picnic guy, but when he told me he had something upstairs in his fraternity room he wanted to show me, somehow I knew I could trust him. Sure enough, he showed me the very first personal computer I'd ever seen that didn't belong to a school or business. It was a little tan cube — an original Macintosh. "Why would you need your own computer?" I asked. "You can just go to the computer lab on campus." With his inner geek bubbling to the surface, he started to explain there'd be a day when everyone would have their own computer, and they'd be small enough to carry around.

I was stunned. "This is, like, totally rad and awesome, dude." Then, we talked about the space shuttle explosion, the football team and President Reagan. The guy knew everything — well, almost. He didn't know anything about grits or the Peanut Festival, but seemed trainable. We spent day after day talking about the strangest things, and he made me laugh every time. I also discovered he played piano by ear, which sent me totally over the moon.

Bob went on to work for Apple Computer, then started his own software company before launching into other techie things. Now, I help him dress and tell him not to put pens in his shirt pocket or tape on his glasses, and in exchange, he helps me with all my computer problems and programs the TV. And the best part is, he also looks dreamy in a white dinner jacket.

So girls, please remember, when a boy shows up at your door with a pen in his pocket, give him a chance. He may just be your perfect mystery date after all.

THE POWER OF A SOFT HANKIE

I've discovered a way to defuse argumentative tempers in meetings and amongst friends. After years of observing wise women, I adopted the practice of carrying a beautiful cotton handkerchief. In this case, softness is truly power.

Reaching for a real cotton handkerchief in a time of crisis can bring animated conversation to a screeching halt. Loud, scary people clam up, because after my tiny "ahem" into the daisy-embellished cloth, they become distracted as they foolishly realize they only have their nasty hands or awkward sleeve for choking episodes.

Between my husband's two grandmothers and mine, many of my dainty cotton squares have an "M" monogram for "Mary," "Minnie," or the other "Mary." The fourth granny's name began with an "E," and I don't have any of hers (note to self: check my cousin's "chester drawers"). Decorated with flowers and crocheted lace edges, there's one to match just about every occasion, including a specific Advent wreath pattern as well as a green shamrock motif.

It's essential that I carry some sort of eye-sopping device

because I cry easily — mostly for happy reasons, but my eyes also tear up from general pollen, bright sun, wind, sneezing and being forced to listen to Neil Diamond for more than a minute.

Skinny dogs taking "naps" on the side of the road bring tears, and saying goodbye to friends sucks the breath out of me. Mean people make me cry frustrated tears, and seeing white shoes before Easter makes me weepy for the loss of civilization as we know it.

On the happier side, I always need a hankie when I smell smoke from birthday candles or hear gravel crunch beneath tires. The color guard leading a parade makes patriotic tears roll down my cheeks, and of course, videos of servicemen and women coming home and surprising their children is a big choke-up. Last week, friends at lunch pulled out my favorite kind of tears — the ones mixed with laughter — and a few days later in church, it was a one-two punch with both "Holy, Holy, Holy" and "Be Thou My Vision" sung on the same morning by an enthusiastic congregation in full harmony. We sang every single verse, including the often-shunned third, and tossed in a powerful key change at the end, so the hankie was soaked.

And lest you think I produce a hankie only when tears are streaming down my face, they've also saved the day when I had to wipe a dirty child's face, dab his skinned knee and mop ice-cream drips off my car seat. A lovely and practical device, no doubt.

Paper tissues are rough and eventually shred to pieces, reminding me of the shredded tissue my fourth-grade teacher tucked in her giant bosom. Yet another reason I prefer cotton.

People gasp when I whip out the little handkerchief, and they can't seem to move. So stunned I'd actually have time to rifle through their pockets before they came to their senses, they finally regain the ability to speak and almost always say the same thing, "That's so pretty. I have some at home. It really makes sense. I should carry a handkerchief."

One of my first little-girl chores around the house was ironing Daddy's handkerchiefs. He always tucked one in his suit pocket and looked very handsome. My husband knows all the ways to fold a man's pocket square, including the crisp fold that really could be used to fling through the air and put someone's eye out like James Bond — yet another useful way to quiet the unruly riffraff in the room and defend yourself with proper hankie.

A delicate antique hankie, once sprinkled with a grandmother's tears and decorated with pastel flowers, is soft enough to comfort, yet strong enough to send a message. When the hankie comes out, you know you're dealing with a modern woman who is prepared for anything.

THE HAND DROP

First steps, first words and first days of school are happy markers in life, but what about when something happens for the last time? Do we even realize what's happening?

The moment he pulled his hand away, I knew I was experiencing a significant last. It hurt so badly I almost choked, but I held it together the day my son last held my hand — or so I thought.

I went to Harrison's elementary school to pick him up early for a dentist appointment. He must have been in the third or fourth grade and came bounding into the front office ready to go, except he remembered at the last second there was a book he needed. He said, "Walk with me to the classroom and I'll show you my art project." He was so happy and grabbed my hand and chattered away as we walked down the corridor lined with construction paper lions with curlicue manes.

Another class of children walking in a line as straight as popcorn approached, and that's when it happened. His little fingers went stiff and his hand was straight like a board. I was dumped right next to the water fountain at Possum Holler Elementary School.

I didn't see it coming, and he gave me no hint this was the direction he was taking. Wanting his freedom at nine years old, he left me hanging, clinging to air. It felt like a thunderstorm.

My heart dropped, because I knew exactly what was going on, but I kept a brave face and didn't comment. Didn't he understand I needed to hold his hand for the rest of his life? He was so adorable, and I needed to have that little bit of connection while he was still little and then maybe even again when he was walking across the stage at high-school graduation.

When he finally grew into a giant college kid, we took him to visit Italy, where everyone holds hands and walks arm in arm. At first, our boys thought it was strange, but eventually, when they saw a grown father and son walking arm in arm and schoolgirls and ladies on their way to lunch, and old nanas with their middle-aged daughters holding tightly to each other and strolling down rough cobblestone streets, Harrison took notice and offered me his hand, which was now much larger and stronger than mine. It felt like sunshine.

I did the mom-swoon and had dreamy eyes with little hearts for pupils. It made up for being dumped all those years before under the fluorescent lights in the school that smelled like cafeteria rolls and sweat.

I realized part of his plan for keeping a firm grip on me was to keep me moving and prevent me from stopping to look in every single store window, but it was also to keep me from twisting my ankles on the cobblestones. And I know good and well that, deep down inside, it was also an excuse to be my little kid again and hold his mom's hand.

The school was big, and he was small, so I held his hand for love and protection. And now the world is large and I am small, and he continues to let me hold on to him for the same exact reasons.

THE DEATH OF THE CHURCH DIRECTORY

Dearly beloved, bow your heads for a moment of silence, because the church directory has bitten the dust. Technology has killed yet another beautiful custom found not exclusively in the South, but one that is certainly treasured and adored by those within our genteel region.

If you walked into your friend's house and there was a church directory on the kitchen counter, you knew you were in the company of good people. All denominations had their own method of listing church members. Some started with a simple typed list of names, addresses and phone numbers, then the Presbyterians got fancy and started using photos, so the Methodists upped them one and used color photos, and finally the Baptists booked a solid week of appointments at the Olan Mills. From there, all the churches in town competed to make their directories look like slick big-city magazines.

Used to start the prayer chains, organize circle meetings, delegate Jell-O salad and casserole duties, and address wedding invitations, the church directory was always close at hand.

I heard my friend Chuck was under the weather, so I wanted

to give him a call. I tried to use the new app on my phone, cleverly called "church directory," only to discover Chuck and his wife weren't listed. The greatest generation isn't always so great at uploading, downloading, swiping and clicking. Instead, I pulled out my old church directory from the last time it was printed in a real paper form, and there were Chuck and his wife, smiling for the camera, with their names, address and phone number in plain sight.

There are plans to update to a newer app where everyone is automatically listed, but until then, the old directory is still useful. Knowing inclusion in the local book may somehow be linked to The Book of Life itself, we are troubled over those not listed, and plan on taking them a Bundt cake as soon as possible.

My friend Penelope Stapleton-Staples, of the Crestview Stapletons, grew up privileged and complained about having to sit for her portrait by the renowned artist from Bogalusa, Vangeaux, who mixed five different shades of yellow to match the exact tones of Penny's golden curls. On the other extreme, my official childhood portrait involved the faux bookcase at Olan Mills, when we went to have our pictures snapped for the church directory.

There was no worse form of torture than Olan Mills church directory day. We dreaded it all year. My father, who was on the church staff, hated going to Olan Mills with a passion. Not because of the harsh lighting or the plastic wagon wheel we had to lean on, but because the photographers always used a baby voice and tried to touch his hair.

Being a minister, Daddy recognized all the signs tempting him to lose control in the whiny voice that would say, "How are we doing today? Don't we want to smoothy-woothy our cowlick?" Daddy had no cowlick at all, and would whip out his small plastic comb, kept in his inside coat pocket, and re-smooth every last hair on his head. But the photographer couldn't control herself and would have to reach out and touch his hair. My brother and I would catch our breath and shudder, thinking of the wrath that was brewing. Our photo in the church directory always looked like we had weapons pointed at our heads . . . and peace be with you, also.

The covers from the directories have long been torn away and lost from my collection of books from different churches in different cities, and the photos within reflect faces that are now older, or completely gone. The pages hold memories of sitting next to friends who harmonized with me, held my hand while I cried, passed me mints when I coughed and loved my children even when they were thumping their feet on the pews. Holding the thin paperbacks and flipping through the worn pages is a simple joy my children will never know. The bound and printed copy of our church history has changed with the times, but somehow, with a little effort, I can still picture the smiling faces of my family of faith.

THE COLORFUL SOUTH

The South may not have the spectacular autumn colors that the Northeast boasts, but what we lack in natural brightness, God makes up for with colorful Southern people.

Southern women are known for wearing bright and bold clothing. Visiting New York City for the first time, I couldn't find a hint of pink, lavender or orange in anyone's clothes. In my small town, they'll actually ask who died if you show up wearing all black before sundown. A Southern woman's closet is like a Crayola box with bright, colorful outfits. We accessorize with bright pocketbooks, shoes, scarves, jewelry and hats to match. We give our favorite men plaid shirts in every collegiate color combination possible, and they look dreamy, if we say so ourselves.

"Why did you get another black swimsuit?" my husband asked.

"That's just about all they sell these days. Someone decided it makes us look slender, so ladies are demanding black swimsuits."

He quickly replied, "Whales are black, and they don't fool me a bit." Great point, and a good reason to exchange that black suit for one that was electric blue.

Southern ladies are a colorful bunch because we have to

compete with azaleas, camellias and crepe myrtles. We have to stand next to majorettes, watermelon queens and along the coast, Mardi Gras floats. We live in a colorful place and use colorful language. Southerners tell colorful stories, and eat colorful foods like orange crawdads, turnip greens, drippy red barbecue sauce, homegrown tomatoes and sweet potato pie. We just love to match the colorful world around us and would get lost in too much beige and taupe, which may lead to our biggest fear . . . blending in.

When Vera Faye came down with heart problems, her doctor, originally from Macon, broke the news so sweetly, she said, "it sounded almost like poetry — so I asked him to tell me again." Our colorful language can be blinding neon, yet melodic and pastel when needed.

I organize my closet by color, left to right, beginning with Easter white and moving over to funeral black. Just by a quick glance, I can tell you I own too many blue things, but hardly any pale yellow since it makes me look sick and people start to fan me when I wear it. "Honey, you need to go lie down for a spell."

"No thank you, it's just this yellow dress. I feel fine." Then I go home and toss the blasted dress in a heap on the floor to punish it for making me look so awful and vow to never buy pale yellow again, no matter what kind of sale Dillard's is having.

The spectacular colors of autumn may not be as vivid in our Southern home as they are in the Northeast, but in a few weeks, we'll make up for our lack of fall color with dazzling Christmas displays that will rival the lights in Times Square. The Bethlehem star had nothing on a Southern woman at Christmastime. We can dazzle and shine and celebrate life with the best of them, all in full, spirited, joyful, bodacious living color.

A
WELL-BALANCED
LOVE

On my way to visit a friend in Georgia, I realized I forgot my toothbrush. I pulled into a drugstore to buy a new pink one because being greeted by a pink toothbrush every morning always makes me happy. It's the little details that make life good, right?

Dodging big-city traffic, I searched for a parking spot in the unfamiliar lot and turned right too soon, which my husband always fusses at me for doing, and may have gently-barely bumped a cement curb.

By the time I drove home to Alabama a few days later, the car was a bit wobbly, but when I peeked underneath, everything looked fine. I figured it would all eventually pop back into place, like our backs do when we reach a certain age (so I've heard).

A day or two later, we were on our way to a fabulous party, or to Sonic, I can't really remember, and Bob hopped behind the wheel of my car. We had only driven about ten feet when he slammed on the brakes and said a more colorful and stronger version of, "Wow, my precious darling! What in the world is that noise? Did you hit something?"

"Well . . ." I started. "You know how many potholes there are in Atlanta. I may have hit one of those on the way home" (a true statement). He cleverly avoided my gaze, because he's experienced the power of my eye trick, taught to me by generations of Southern women and perfected by studying Kaa, the snake on *The Jungle Book*.

Then I whispered, "They really should fix those roads. Humph! Georgia!"

He pulled back into the driveway and said with his really awesome deep voice, "Leslie Anne, you know you're eventually going to tell me the truth, so you may as well tell me now."

Bob knows my weakness is being too honest and I can't really hold a fib in very long. Believe me, I've tried. (Don't ever tell me about a surprise party.) I kind of admire real liars for their crafty steadfastness. He knew the truth would ultimately tumble out but didn't want to wait.

I began with the part about forgetting the toothbrush, mentioned the ill-placed curb, may or may not have blamed a Georgia Tech engineer, and ended with, "They didn't even have pink. I had to settle for green. Who in the world would brush their teeth with a green toothbrush?"

The next day, Bob gave up his time to have my car fixed, which turned out to be both a damaged tire and a bent wheel. Just to keep me safe, he had the garage install not one but four new tires. My car drove like a magic carpet.

Husbands are supposed to love their wives like Christ loved his earthly body of believers — the church. And when this is put into action, it demonstrates abundant, overflowing grace.

God knows our weaknesses, yet encourages us to stick with what is true, noble, right, pure and lovely. Even though we're guilty of wrongdoing, when we deserve wrath, He offers grace and forgiveness. When we need one tire, God gives us four. Overflowing with bountiful love, God reaches down and takes care of our mess. And when someone on earth loves you that way, it's an amazing thing that makes life feel well balanced.

THE BIRTH OF A SOUTHERN BABY

Although I think it's crass to publicly discuss personal things such as childbirth, finances or your sister-in-law's dress size, I'm finally old enough to have friends who are becoming grandparents, and all they want to talk about is childbirth, as if it's something new.

This baby chatter has made me recall a few things about my own experience that are acceptable for conversation, and who knows? It may just help other expectant mothers focus on what is really important.

Twenty years ago, the gospel of *What to Expect When You Are Expecting* encouraged us to choose a "birthing song" to accompany the event, as if it were going to be choreographed and the baby was going to show up dancing. I think it was mainly for the entertainment of the nursing staff, but they acted like the baby couldn't be born if we didn't have a CD player to blast out our baby's official song.

Since both boys were born in the shadow of Georgia's Kennesaw Mountain National Battlefield, I naturally chose "American Trilogy" by Elvis. A little "Dixie" followed by "The Battle Hymn of the Republic" and "All My Trials" — what battlefield baby wouldn't like that? No one besides Superman can rock a cape like Elvis, and the song contained the all-important majestic key change needed to introduce a baby to Georgia.

As it turned out, since I'd never had a baby before, I didn't know what I'd really want was total silence. Noise of any kind suddenly drove me out of my mind, so Elvis was hushed and my husband had to give up his convenient yet irritatingly squeaky rolling padded seat. Poor guy. He was very uncomfortable having to stand. My heart broke for him.

I wore pearls, because I was afraid the baby wouldn't recognize me otherwise, and added my diamond stud earrings on the way out the door, because it was, after all, a very special occasion and properly after sundown.

The regular hospital gown wouldn't do, because who knows what kind of criminal element could have worn it before me? No amount of scalding water can cleanse bad vibes, so I had permission to wear my own Brooks Brothers gown in navy blue to compliment my eyes, since I didn't want to meet my son looking haggard or washed out.

Willadean bragged that her daughter-in -law was going to have a natural no-drug-organic childbirth. I guess she also refuses Novocain at the dentist's office and shuns coffee in the mornings?

When the bill from my anesthesiologist arrived, I paid it right away and gave him a generous tip. A little over three years later, when our second was born, the same anesthesiologist walked into the room and I said, "I've been dreaming about you for the last three months."

Perhaps I need to hang around my younger friends who aren't reliving their childbirth experiences, because I'm having too much fun right now with no babies or teens in the house. I keep electrical cords dangling from the wall, sharp objects and tiny doo-dads in glass dishes scattered around on low tables and cook food full of spicy gluten and allergy-inducing peanuts. I don't cut my grapes in half, and I keep my poisons down low in unlocked cabinets. When my friends email me photos of a drooling tot, I just sit back and remember my Elvis birthing song . . . "Glory, glory hallelujah — no more babies in the house." I knew that song would eventually come in handy.

MUSIC APPRECIATION

My husband and I shared a sideways glance and silently mouthed a name that was loaded with low-class geekiness. We were listening to a live opera performance in the home of Vivaldi and Rossini, no less, and the name we whispered was "Bugs Bunny." You can force the kids to grow up and let them roam around the world, but our American musical heritage will stay with us forever. Even if it was delivered by Saturday morning cartoons.

With genius like "The Rabbit of Seville" ("Welcome to my shop, let me cut your mop"), *The Pink Panther*, and my favorite, *Mr. Rogers' Neighborhood*, is it any wonder we found our classical and jazz music roots in childhood TV?

Jazz didn't get any better than the live music from Johnny Costa in Mr. Rogers' living room. We didn't realize there was a grand piano just off camera where the famous Pittsburgh pianist would improvise. Critics predicted the style would be too advanced for children, yet the smooth background somehow fit the show perfectly. We loved Mr. Rogers' music and found it compatible with the rolling fun of Vince Guaraldi's work on

Peanuts. Charlie Brown may have been awkward, but his life's soundtrack was pure elegance.

We didn't realize we were scampering out of bed on Saturday mornings to listen to one of the greatest composers in the world, Henry Mancini. But that panther — man, he was so cool. (The aardvark spoiled it all.)

It's no wonder that as grown-up parents, we cringed at a singing purple dinosaur. Our soundtrack of childhood was far more sophisticated than we realized, and something was not quite right with this new generation of repetitive whining.

Our friend Mr. Rogers not only provided great music but also introduced us to superstars like Wynton and Branford Marsalis, Yo-Yo Ma, and Tony Bennett. I remember watching an episode where he interviewed a harpist, which convinced me I was destined to play the harp. My parents explained it wouldn't fit into our Volkswagen, so they quickly bought me a flute instead.

By the time my children were born, TV shows had devolved into 30 minutes of flashy squeaks and squawks, so I carefully monitored their shows. I even nixed a show that most parents felt was the only way possible for children to learn the alphabet. It was too flashy and had terrible music, so the green guy in the garbage can got canned at our house. But when it was nap time, I'd pop in a classical CD and tell them the name of the piece and composer. I wasn't sure if they were understanding me or not until my son told me, "No Pro-kef! (Prokofiev) Peter and Wolf — scary!" And while sitting at the circus, he excitedly announced, "Hey! That's *Carmen*, by Bizet!

Little brains are sponges. If we provide anxiety-producing computerized junk, that's what will fill their brains. If we offer them beauty, tranquility and substance, they'll give it back to us with overflowing ingenuity and imagination.

Children need exposure to quality music, not just for their

creative process but also for developing their language, social and math skills. And let's face it: familiarity with a few famous operas and symphonies also comes in handy when you want to impress your husband with your *Looney Tunes* repertoire.

PARTY WITH A PUNCHBOWL

I've discovered you can tell a lot about a person by their reaction to a punchbowl.

Accepting a small cup of punch by saying "thank you" is a sign you've been raised right. Shouting "Hey! Look at these little cups! Is this supposed to be all I get to drink?" is a sign that you . . . well, it's a sign you won't be invited back.

Like a deviled-egg plate or a string of pearls, every true Southern woman has a punchbowl, probably passed down from a relative or given as a wedding gift. Punchbowls usually spend most of the year on top of the extra refrigerator in the laundry room or on a top shelf in the pantry, but when we need them, they are ready for action.

Our parties are as varied as the people who live here. We host formal dinners, children's birthday parties, cookouts (never called a "barbecue," which is a type of food), shindigs, soirees and hoedowns. The occasional hootenanny is never really planned but usually begins as an innocent Bunco game. It switches gears when Mara Mae wants to show everyone pictures of her ex's new wife and someone realizes it's their old sorority sister. Suddenly, your neighbor is standing on a chair pantomiming something that happened in Gulf Shores in 1986, and it all goes downhill from there. That's a hootenanny, and no punchbowl is required.

Whether you're hosting a prayer group supper, retirement reception, or even a baby shower with crepe-paper streamers, the level of frivolity and excitement always gets bumped up a notch when you pull out your punchbowl. People go crazy over the tiny cups, and most appreciate that you've color coordinated the punch to match your décor. Of course, there's no need to say it, because you already know, if it's a wedding reception, you match the punch to the bridesmaids' dresses. If this is news to you, let me take this opportunity to welcome you to the South.

Like most of you, I know about three basic recipes for punch by heart, but I always like to check the measurements so as not to overload it with too much pineapple juice or ginger ale. I pulled out my old church cookbook because I needed a nonalcoholic version for those who may be "weak for the drink." The only version of punch I found that looked good was submitted by a good friend, Mrs. Hayes, but it was for a crowd of 150. I didn't feel like doing the math to scale it down to only 30, so I went to the next cookbook that was sure to have an appropriate clean-as-a-whistle recipe, *Baptist Dishes Worth Blessing*, copyrighted 1978 by The New Orleans Baptist Theological Seminary — you can't go wrong with that.

About 25 or so recipes were listed after a page of reminders like "1 pound of coffee plus 2 gallons of water equals 40 cups of coffee." The first recipe listed was a definite no. Frozen banana punch. Yuck, no thanks. But the next entry, by Mrs. Melvin J. Poole (Linda), was perfect. Lime punch would match my Christmas table, and I already had lime Jell-O on my Jell-O shelf, but then again, who doesn't?

There was no better punch ever tasted than the champagne

punch made and served by the much-beloved Bucky at the Grand Hotel in Point Clear, Alabama. For years, Bucky was known to remember everyone's name and would hand you a cold cup of punch while you waited in the lobby for Sunday brunch. He always knew to offer a half-filled cup of the squeaky-clean version to the children, so as not to exclude them from the fun, and the children would eye the little silver cups with pride, thinking they were big enough to drink punch like a grown-up. It also forced them to stand still with their parents, which may have been Bucky's main motive all along.

For extra flair, I had time to freeze a portion of the punch in a little ring, with bright red cherries dotting the top. If I needed a talent for a beauty pageant, I just might stand onstage and plop a molded ice ring into a bowl of punch. With just enough flair, yet minimal splash, ta-da! The judges would go wild.

Special occasions in the South bounce all over the place as far as formality and decorations go. I've seen grown men dip fruity beverages out of a lined garbage can at ten o'clock in the morning while they load their "throws" on a Mardi Gras float, and someone once put their bottled beverages in an old wooden canoe filled with ice. Clean clear crisp water to hard hot hooch — it's all served around here at one time or another.

But no matter what is served or how, there's a certain dignity the punchbowl lends. It's like having your grandmother walk into the room. People stand up straighter, speak in hushed tones and remember their manners. No wonder punchbowls are used for cotillion dances. It calms all those seventh graders down and forces them to practice the most civilized opening line ever: "Would you care for some punch?"

HUGGERS VS. HANDSHAKERS

I'm a hugger — but a hugger who would really and truly rather shake your hand. I hug some people freely, with joy and enthusiasm, but feel it's a status to be earned, not expected. When I see hug-worthy friends, I'll gladly throw myself into their arms, while others warrant a warm smile, friendly handshake, or in some situations the lethal Southern-lady weapon of a cold stare.

If you've been around teenaged girls lately, you know it's like a barrel of otters with all the squirming and hugging going on. While chaperoning a group of teens I noticed the girls hugged each other every few minutes. "Hugsies!" one girl screamed as she launched herself into the middle of a group. Do their parents think this ear-piercing squealing and over-hugging behavior is cute? And once again, I say, "Thank you, God, for giving me boys."

Southerners will say, "Let me hug your neck," or "Give me some sugar," which is usually directed at kinfolk. I think it's the newcomers who are introducing the hug-everyone-in-the-world concept. My New Jersey husband says everyone up there hugs and kisses each other whether they're close or not.

My mom's Irish family hugged, but not excessively. My dad's

British family excelled at the handshake. Mother said the first time she met Dad's family when she went home with him in college, Daddy and my grandfather ran towards each other and enthusiastically shook hands. She liked-to-have-died. By the time I was born, she had converted them to huggers, but with my DNA test reporting I'm 74% British, 14% Scottish, Irish and Welsh, I'm doomed to a lifetime of sunscreen and handshaking.

The list of people I like to hug includes but is not limited to: those who smell really good, puppies, good altos, clean children, people who have been missing for over eight months, anyone who ever helped me with algebra, everyone on Easter and anyone who is wearing an FSU shirt. Bless their hearts, the Seminoles need extra hugs this year.

I loved watching the British characters shake hands on *Downton Abbey*. Even with great excitement, there was no hugging, fist bumping, slapping or tousling hair. Just a big smile and a hearty, "Well done, old chap!"

My husband's Italian family wants to hug and kiss you, then repeat it all over again two minutes later. Even if they're yelling at you, they want to hug, which is very scary for anyone from South Alabama. Once I went to the kitchen to get my husband's grandmother a napkin, and she nearly smothered me, which was hard to do, because she had tiny spaghetti-like arms.

I recently met a man for the first time who reached out and pulled me in for a full-frontal hug, which I found to be quite awkward. I mean, I didn't even know the guy and he got the full tour. Of course, when I pulled away, he was equally rude to mention it: "What? You don't like me?" Which of course is an overeager hugger's way of labeling you as a psychopath. I didn't think anything bad about him but secretly resented his mother for raising such a man. She was probably a teenaged squealing over-hugger in her youth.

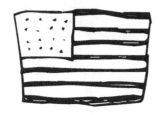

OUT-OF-TOWN
JUDGES

It was an honor to be asked to judge an out-of-town beauty pageant, which nowadays is called a "scholarship competition." Due to the confidentiality agreement, I can't reveal the name of the event, but these young ladies in Central Alabama were dynamos of good grades and good deeds. The top winners earned the honor to ride on the FFA float in the Christmas parade, visit nursing homes and cut grand-opening ribbons.

I can understand the politically correct reasons for eliminating the swimsuit competition, but as someone who has participated in this activity, let me just say, if you show me a young lady who is capable of simultaneously walking in high heels, sucking in her gut, standing in the correct spot and smiling into a blinding spotlight — all while being squeezed, taped, poked and pinned into a swimsuit — you've got a confident woman on your hands. She's the one who will grow up to fight city hall, rescue a litter of puppies and cook dinner for a dozen people, all on the same day. A swimsuit contestant will be the one who will someday snatch her child from the mouth of a lion, smack it on the nose, then save you from a burning building on the way home.

If you asked 100 women if they'd rather walk through a swamp filled with snakes or cross a stage while wearing a swimsuit, 99 of them would choose the swamp. But win or lose, the swimsuit contestant is the one you'll want to have by your side in battle. There's no better test of bravery than a Jantzen and a spotlight.

The swimsuit competition was replaced with a costume contest, which doesn't tell me anything about inner fortitude. It only reveals who has a kindergarten teacher for a mother, due to their graduate-level use of glitter.

Halfway through the evening, I grew bored with all the dramatic readings (doesn't anyone take piano lessons anymore?) until Twila Grace danced with flowy scarves to the Guy Penrod version of "Count Your Blessings." Things almost spun out of control when the next contestant did a ventriloquist act and belted out, "I miss Mayberry, sittin' on the porch drinking iced-cold cherry . . . Coke." The na-na-na part got the poor girl's tongue tangled. She went into a gagging fit and started to spit a little, which was illuminated beneath the glaring lights and made it look like the sprinkler system had been activated. Frustrated and embarrassed, she drop-kicked the dummy into the audience, but everyone thought it was part of a comedy routine and roared with laughter. The last contestant of the night stole the show when she twirled the baton to "Eastbound and Down" from *Smokey and the Bandit* — which I've decided is officially the best baton-twirling song ever.

We awarded the title to the baton twirler because she was cute as a button, and because during the interview she confessed she had borrowed her evening dress to save money, which we all admired.

Hopeful mothers with fingers still encrusted with glitter lingered in the parking lot to question our decision, but the sheriff's deputy escorted us safely to our cars. That's why it's always good to get out-of-town judges.

WHEN SOUTHERN SUMMERS WERE COOL

Summer, Autumn, Winter ("Winnie") and Spring are friends of my sons. Two are adorable, one is a tart, and the other will be a beauty someday — as soon as she grows into her teeth, bless her heart. With absolutely no connection to these young ladies whatsoever, and thinking only of the seasonal calendar, I have to say Summer is my absolute favorite.

The humid air seems thicker, which slows us down a bit more than usual. If your son is (un)fortunate enough to make the All-Star play-offs, you'll sit through the longest, hottest baseball games of your life watching the ball seemingly hang in mid-air while you question if it was really possible you shivered beneath sweaters at the start of the season.

There was a time when we all loved Southern summers. They weren't so hot or humid, they weren't miserable at all. But what was once our favorite time of year has turned into the season of complaints.

Stopping to stare at a rain puddle, you can almost remember how your feet felt cold and slippery when you'd splash in the mud after a rainstorm. You can recall riding bikes and eating popsicles on days when the heat never bothered us. The cold movie theatre would show Batman and Pete's Dragon and we'd drink cherry Slushies till our tongues were frozen, making us talk funny.

We'd catch lightning bugs and small toads for entertainment far better than any video game. Our parents would take us to family reunions where we'd eat chicken and dumplings, deviled eggs, fresh garden peas and then poke our fingers into 15 different cakes.

We'd spend a week with our grandparents and were allowed to play in the creek, pick corn and throw watermelon rinds to the cows. No one worried about us riding in the back of pick-up trucks and the wind would blow through our sticky hair while we laughed and sang with our cousins.

The only time we wanted to wake up early in July was during Vacation Bible School. We'd come home with cheeks stained with purple Kool-Aid and our fingers sticky from gluing popsicle sticks to a milk carton. Our hearts were full of songs about Jesus and we never once mentioned the temperature outside.

But now we say it's hotter than new love and there's no way we can even walk to the mailbox. We buy our tomatoes from the farmer's market because we can't possibly make a garden ourselves in this heat. We tell our children to stay inside and watch movies or play video games because obviously the heat is too much for them. They need to be driven to friend's houses because a bike ride on a day like today would certainly kill them.

But sometimes, around the end of July, we'll hear a song on the radio that reminds us of a day at the beach with sandwiches and icy bottles of Cokes. For a split second, we recall what it was like to be in love with Southern summers. A breeze blowing against our face reminds us of singing into a rotary fan to make robot voices and the chime of our seatbelt makes us look over our shoulder for the ice cream truck.

While my son's friend Summer is cute as a bug in a rug, our real Southern summers are brutal.

Maybe it's not the heat we hate, but instead, it's the lack of carefree days that drives us crazy. When childhood days were sweltering, we'd run through a sprinkler. Now, our legs stick to the nuclear car seats and our shirts cling to our back.

Our homemade ice cream freezers have been replaced with eight dollar smoothies from a drive-thru and our Slip 'N Slides have been traded for phones loaded with mindless games. It's not the heat or humidity. It's not the frizzy hair or crowds at the beach. What makes us dread summers now is that we've forgotten how to enjoy them. Southern summers were made for playing. They were given to us as a little treat for enduring the rest of the serious year. Summertime was created for children and those who are still young at heart.

SCENTS AND SENSIBILITY

Loyalty is a well-known characteristic of Southerners, and just as they are loyal to china patterns and sororities, Southern ladies are also deeply devoted to their perfumes. Our signature scents speak more about us than who our people are, because while we can't choose our relatives, good breeding teaches us to take great care when selecting our perfume.

If your family has been in the South long enough to have had a cannonball-landing-on-the-front-porch story, then chances are, your great-great (etc.) granny dabbed a little bit of vanilla behind her ear while she was baking a pound cake, just before Pa came in from plowing the field. Generations of Southern women have perfected the art of flirting and know that, after the stomach, the way to a man's heart is through his nose.

Smelling good isn't just for romance. When returning home from college, my son scoops me up and always comments, "Mmm, you smell good!" He could be relating what he smells to his favorite meals I cook or the perfume I wore when I would hold him and read *The Little Engine That Could*. Whatever it is he detects, it always makes me feel good that he notices.

Women worldwide love to smell good, but Southern ladies put more thought and effort into the process because we're under pressure to compete with our intoxicating environment of magnolias, gardenias and jasmine, not to mention the good-smelling food coming out of kitchens all up and down the street.

Early training taught my generation to start our scented journey on pink bottles of Love's Baby Soft while we'd also sneak spritzes of our mothers' Charlie and Shalimar.

My two grandmothers are not only eternally linked to their signature "toilet waters," which cracked me up as a little girl, but also to the scents of their soaps. One was loyal to Ivory, the other to Dove. I can still unwrap a bar of one of these soaps and instantly think I'm right there in their house again.

Wanting to be unique and not smell like every other woman at the PTA meetings, I shunned the ultra-popular Chanel No. 5 and instead opted for the more elusive Chanel No. 22, therefore making me a wild rebel. But to my horror, they discontinued the light and powdery No. 22 in the United States. I simply had to travel to Europe in order to find my signature scent, but alas, my husband didn't think this was reason enough to jet off to Paris or Milan.

While I conducted the very important search for a new scent, my friend Mary Sue gave me a gift basket filled with fun little trinkets, and amongst the pens, candles and candies, she included a little spray bottle of body mist. I recognized it as one of the inexpensive drugstore sprays. But I wasn't picky, especially since I didn't have any more of the Chanel No. 22, so I tried it and loved it. A hint of cinnamon, vanilla and something else I couldn't identify — it was heavenly. Almost like a warm cookie.

I got in the habit of spritzing on just a little bit of the body spritz from the plastic bottle every morning, and people around me went wild. I'd never had so many compliments on my perfume, and total strangers would ask me what it was. I didn't try to put on airs, and openly admitted it was an inexpensive drugstore spray.

Everyone was very impressed with both my delightful, alluring scent and down-to-earth frugality.

Seeing Mary Sue at a bridal shower, I had to tell her how much I loved the new scent, but she had no idea what I was talking about. "I never give perfume to other people because it's such a personal choice," she explained.

"I'm sure you just forgot," I told her. "It was a plastic bottle about this high, with a picture of a flower on the front," I reminded her.

Mary Sue had a strange look come over her face, then as good friends do, discreetly leaned over and whispered, "That wasn't perfume. It was air freshener." It seems the flower on the label really was a vanilla bean in bloom and the spray really was supposed to smell like a freshly baked cookie.

"Oh, dear God in heaven, help me now, and save me from myself and my poor eyesight!" I had been walking around for weeks with cookie-scented air freshener spritzed on my wrists and neck. Mary Sue and I laughed so hard we almost spilled our little silver teacups of pink strawberry-sherbet punch.

I've finally settled on a new signature scent, found here in the United States — readily available in the cosmetic department at Dillard's, to be exact. I no longer confuse the perfume with the air freshener. And when my son returns home for a visit, he tells me how good I smell, then raves about how the powder room smells wonderful . . . just like warm cookies.

IT'S NOT GOSSIP IF IT'S A PRAYER REQUEST

Daisy Dee burst into the coffee shop, ran over to our table and whispered, "Y'all, pray for Bernice. She's back on her nerve pills, all on account of her daughter Vernice wanting to hold her wedding at the Buc-ee's on I-10."

Daisy Dee was following the Southern rule of "if it's a prayer request, it's not gossip." Kind of like on *Jeopardy!*, where answers have to be given in the form of a question, gossip around here has to be in the form of a prayer request, or else you'll be . . . you know, sinning, and that's a step beyond tacky.

To add the final spit and polish of righteousness, Daisy Dee added, "Bless her heart."

"Yes," we all said in unison, "bless her heart."

"I'll pray for her," said Roo Anne.

"As will I," said Pauleena.

"Well, I'm going to call her and ask if the wedding cake will have little beef jerky sprinkles on top," said Penelope.

"Penny! You can't be serious. Don't do that!"

"Oh, you know I was just kidding," she said.

"We'll pray for you too," called out Daisy Dee as she swished to the counter to order a caramel sugar-free, fat-free, gluten-free, low-caffeine Ice-Rageous.

The Texas-based Buc-ee's is a mega gas station/rest stop/ snacking hall of fame that just opened its doors in Robertsdale, Alabama, and is already the talk of the state. Low gas prices, T-shirts, cast-iron skillets, stuffed beaver toys and the self-proclaimed cleanest restrooms this side of your mama's house. How could we not text each other later that day and say, "Buc-ee's? Really? LOL — WOW! Help me!" but we added little prayer-hand emojis so it was still in the form of a proper prayer.

When I was in the sixth grade, a high-school boy went to the altar at the end of the Sunday night service. The pastor said, "Son, we're glad you're here tonight. God hears your prayers."

With that encouragement, the teen started pouring out his heart. "I'm sorry I've been fooling around with . . ." and from there, the list of girls' names started to flow. Girls started crying, mothers clutched their pearls and daddies slammed their hymnals closed.

The pastor finally gained control and said, "Let us pray," which in this situation was code for, "Close your eyes, I'll say the fastest prayer known to man, and we'll all be home eating Ritz crackers and cheese within 15 minutes."

The boy's mother later said, "What's the big deal? Those girls were chasing him and he just needed prayer." See what she did? She turned the gossip into a prayer request.

Being nominated for the church prayer chain is an honor that means you are truly righteous and can pray away arguments, termites, a string of car burglaries, foul-mouthed children and general evil. It also means you can keep a secret, because there's nothing worse than notifying the prayer chain that you are standing in the need of prayer only to find it posted on social media 20 minutes later. Churches that openly allow just anyone to sign up for the prayer chain are attracting the gossips like gnats to a cur dog.

Penelope was asked to join but politely declined. She confessed, "I told them I was too busy, but I really knew my head would explode with all that inside information." I think God loves her for her honesty. Just like he'll love me for declining the wedding invitation at Buc-ee's. It would just be too much for me to hold inside. Bless my own honest heart, and please pray.

HOME IN A JAR

I have a jar of white sand I scooped up from my parents' house the last time I was there. Surrounded by citrus trees my dad planted, the house was only a short walk from the Santa Rosa Sound, where you could look across the water and see the barrier island that protected them from the Gulf of Mexico and fierce tropical storms.

Although I never lived in that house, my boys grew up playing on the small protected beach, where magnolias and cabbage palms shaded their fair skin and the waves were gentle and free from stinging sea creatures. It was Old Florida, out of sight of condos and amusement parks, with a pier for fishing and tossing out crab traps.

After my father passed away, my mother's plan was to stay in the house for a few years. Yet after only a few months, she decided to move to a place near her favorite child (don't show this to my brother).

Thus began the months of agony that many families know, sorting, packing, giving away, selling and emptying out box after box of memories. As kindergarten teachers know, "I just might need this someday" was my mother's professional oath she swore, with one hand on her heart and the other on a Dick and Jane reader. We found wooden thread spools and buttons and keys used for math activities. There was the Holy Grail of Early Childhood Education — a bag of toilet paper rolls — the sign of an excellent teacher, and of course, lots of books and puppets. After rescuing my own sweet dolls and school yearbooks, we gave the rest to appreciative new teachers and children. My prayer of thanks that got me through the move was, "Thank you, Lord, that she never wanted to collect Hummel figurines, which would have been the sure death of me."

With or without an actual structure on the property, we can tell the story of how there used to be a house, a farm or a family that filled the air with laughter, tears and shrieks of joy. Little boys, babies and brides all walked beneath the trees, and yet now, there's an empty field, parking lot or new house — never as wonderful as the original.

Eventually, our former houses look smaller and the trees larger. A new family lives there, but we don't want to bother strangers — but how can they be strangers if we dance across the same stage of memories? Are their children sliding down the same staircase? Do they see our rainbow on the wall on sunny afternoons? Are they growing tomatoes in the same fertile spot?

It's just a house, not our home, because home is where our heart is. Still, we will always close our eyes and picture Christmas trees, backyard picnics and friends swinging on the porch. Unable to pack these things in a box, we instead keep pressed satsuma blossoms in our Bible, door keys on blue ribbons tucked in a drawer and jars of sand on our desk. These small handheld treasures make the heart-held memories come alive and, for a moment, seem real again.

HELLO LESSONS

Our elder son was a bit shy, or so we thought until we discovered he was, more accurately, stubborn. When a man at church stopped, leaned down, and asked, "What's your name?" our son stared straight at him with no emotion whatsoever.

"Tell Mr. McGibby what your name is," we coached. Still, our darling little redhead looked straight ahead, mute and in a trance.

"Oh, I guess he's just shy," said our friend, which made our son look relieved.

As soon as Mr. McGibby was out of sight, our three year old looked at us with a wry little smile and said, "I say nothing to that man!" It was a statement of triumph and victory, not remorse or shame.

We discovered at that moment our son was on a path of loving extreme control, and we were on a path to pulling our hair out. He had skipped the terrible twos, and at three was just starting to exert his baby-control. It was a battle that would last for . . . well, he's 21 now, so that long. Our recent text exchange with the college senior went something like this:

"I don't want to walk in the graduation ceremony."

"Walk, or else we'll pull you across the stage in a wagon!"

"But the cap and gown is going to be so hot!"

"We paid extra for a college with air-conditioning. Sign up now."

"Maybe."

Not ones to be outsmarted by a toddler, my husband and I took charge of the situation by explaining what it meant to have polite conversations. From then on, toddler-boy was expected to look adults in their eyes, smile and speak kindly. No excuses, no shyness cop-out. We explained it's okay to be on the quiet side, but not speaking to someone when they address you is rude. Even the shyest of children need to know how to properly greet another person, especially an adult. They may be three years old today, but in the blink of an eye, they'll be on a job interview.

After we laid down the law, if "lil'guy" failed to be polite to adults who spoke to him by at least acknowledging them, we had to have a "practice" when we got home. We'd say, "We're so sorry you forgot to use your good manners when Mrs. Frillypants spoke to you, so I guess you need to practice saying hello." We'd then stand in front of him and pretend to be a kind person who said, "Hello, little guy. How are you today?" If he failed to respond acceptably, we'd say, "Okay, let's try again." We'd role play until he was bored and itching to play with his toys. We made the practice sessions serious, and as dull as possible. Our little student quickly learned he'd better be polite and respectful, or else he'd have to endure "hello lessons" when we got home.

Over the years, I've heard countless parents say in front of their children, "Oh, she's shy, she won't talk to you." Or something along the lines of, "He hates to read," "She can't carry a tune in a bucket," or "He never eats anything green." These kiddies are listening with big ears and turning our statements into excuses for failure and self-fulfilling prophecies. Bad behavior and bad habits are often reflections of the parents' assumptions and excuses.

"We can't make little Darla Jean keep her clothes on, ha-ha-ha! Look at her go!" Well, precious tootsie takes the statement as permission, so she's off the hook to act acceptably, and to a child, freedom feels oh-so-great. If Mama says it, it must be true. "Go, Darla Jean, go!"

It wasn't until our son was in middle school when someone finally told us how polite he was and that he shook their hand and spoke respectfully while looking them in the eye. "Are you sure it was our son?" we asked.

Sure, some children really are naturally shy, but even they need to learn the value of treating others with respect and dignity. Someday they'll realize that social skills really do come in handy every now and then.

Of course, the way nature works, beginning at age two, our next son wouldn't stop walking up to strangers, shaking their hands and talking their ears off, resulting in our having to give him "stranger danger" lessons.

COLLEGE — WHAT ARE YOU GOING TO DO ABOUT IT?

Attention, all parents who are planning on launching a child off to college next fall — if they don't already know how to do their own laundry, make a basic pot of mac and cheese and sew a button on their shirt, you are officially in danger of becoming one of "those" parents, and worse yet, your precious collegiate darling will be one of "those" kids.

Training your young Jedi to lead a life of independence begins with the magic phrase, "What are you going to do about it?"

"Mom! My green dress is wrinkled!"

"Hmm. What are you going to do about it?" the smart mom replies.

"I have a huge paper due in three days!"

And the clever parent says, "I'll pour you a glass of iced tea while you figure out what you're going to do about it."

Lula Leigh loved her university and pledged a sorority that had pink as one of its official colors, which delighted her to no end. But her happiness was clouded because she accumulated demerits for missing important chapter meetings that taught her how to sing songs and hold a candle at the same time. It seems poor Lula Leigh had never kept her own schedule before. In high school, she relied on mommy dearest to coordinate her activities on a computer, phone, paper and a whiteboard in their kitchen, and now without mommy, Lula Leigh was a lost pink mess.

Speaking of pink, Huck was no better. He had to wear pink socks and shirts every day since he ruined his laundry the first week of college. But he discovered girls love pink, so he was feeling pretty good until his car conked out because he didn't know what to do when those little lights on the dashboard started flashing.

"Slow to launch" is the new name for "spoiled rotten." Seeing parents micromanage and do everything for a teenager, from pouring the milk on their cereal in the morning to negotiating grades with teachers, is shocking.

"I can't find a parking spot." "I'm out of paper for the printer." "There's a bee in my room." These are real phone calls made by (helpless) college freshmen. Instead of asking what they are going to do about it and encouraging them to find a solution, parents have actually jumped in their cars and driven a hundred miles or more to hold their hands and soothe them with a pot of homemade stew. And as long as they're on campus, they may as well clean the dorm room and do the laundry.

Believing life-lesson chores can't start too early, I told my elementary-aged boys that a toilet brush was really just a fluffy light saber with magical powers to make disgusting toilets gleam like shiny robots. "And if you are very good, I'll also allow you to push the buttons on this very expensive, high-tech machine that will clean your stinky socks. Here's where you pour in the magic chemicals (detergent), and — just listen to that computer inside. It blinks and buzzes just like R2-D2."

When my friends and I started college, our parents dropped us off, gave us a quick hug, then hit the road. Move-in day on campus now is sometimes an entire move-in week, with parents spending their vacation days helping decorate little Tad's room. Dad hangs the television set and artwork while Mom arranges the toiletries on shelves, then they take a break and drink coffee from the espresso bar installed the day before. The truth escapes them that within a month their designer efforts will be covered in old pizza boxes and dirty clothes, exactly like the other rooms — until Mom shows up a day early for Homecoming and tidies things up a bit.

At this point, if your high-school senior doesn't know the difference between a flat head vs. Phillips head, or how to hang a shower curtain or scramble an egg, the question also applies to you — what are you going to do about it? The good news is, you have time for a crash course in independence before next fall. May the force be with you.

GRACE THAT IS GREATER THAN OUR SINS

There needs to be a word to describe the specific feeling you get when you are simultaneously furious with your child and yet still want to hug them till they melt in your arms.

I thought of this when my husband told me, "All the boys in Thailand have been freed from the cave."

"Let the spankings begin," I laughed.

Of course, I was only joking, because I, along with the rest of the world, was immensely relieved and had prayed for them to be released from their underground entrapment. As someone who panics over the thought of being trapped, and as the mother of boys, I was sick with worry about these children who had been stranded in a cave system for nearly three weeks.

When the boys were safely home, the parents probably wanted to say, "Didn't you read the warning signs about flash floods?" "What were you thinking?" "Haven't I told you to stay out of those caves?" "If one friend runs into a cave, does that mean you have to follow?"

Within two seconds flat, they also wanted to add, "You're never leaving my sight again." "I cooked all your favorite foods."

"I love you so much." "You can have that puppy you've been wanting." "We're giving your brother and sister away so we can focus only on you for the rest of our lives."

When my younger son was five years old, I sent him across the street — which was actually a small, safe gravel road — to drop off some cookies for an elderly neighbor. I watched from the kitchen window as he scampered up the steps of her big front porch, then waited for him to return while I busied myself with another chore. It wasn't until about 10 minutes later I realized I hadn't heard him come inside.

I searched our yard, then remembered I saw a scruffy-looking stranger walk down our remote road earlier in the morning. Chills ran down my back. Up and down the street I walked calling my son's name. My neighbors joined in the hunt for my son, who was prone to adventure and exploring. Their help was comforting yet made it more of an official search, which added an uneasy edge to the situation. There was talk of calling the police, but I kept my cool, although hot tears were ready to spill down my cheeks. After about 45 minutes, a friend found my little guy, safe and sound, sitting on our neighbor's sofa eating Jell-O and watching cartoons. Even though I had instructed him not to bother her by going inside, the temptation of a snack and the neighbor's sweetness had pulled him in, and he made himself at home.

I searched for that elusive word to describe my mix of fear, relief, exasperation and joy, but it was far too complicated an emotion to name.

Even as adults, we too can wander away and ignore warnings, only to end up in unexpected trouble. God has every right to be angry with our carelessness and broken hearted by our disobedience, yet like a good parent, overlooks the mistakes and welcomes us into his arms with unconditional love. We may deserve a holy spanking, but instead, God shows us great compassion.

Like the Navy SEALs in Thailand, God can rescue us from the mess we've created and replace his anger with love, demonstrating grace and the beauty of second chances — that's the word I'm looking for . . . grace. Amazing grace made for adventurous absent-minded little boys all over the world, as well as their parents.

IT HAS POCKETS

I attended a charity group's Christmas party last year where most of us were strangers. Even though we were all Southern women and therefore had never met a stranger, conversation was still unexplainably stiff and formal, and there was an awkward silence in the room. But within a few minutes, I uttered the magic words that brought out the chatterbox in us all.

After someone kindly complimented my skirt, I replied, "Thank you . . . it has pockets."

From the immediate gasp and uproar, you'd think I'd said, "Thank you . . . Jesus made it himself."

Eyes suddenly sparkled, ladies jumped from their chairs, hand motions were rapid, and the room exploded with animated conversation. Eggnog sloshed into tiny glass punch cups, and someone hummed Christmas carols. It turned into the best Christmas party of the season.

There's always great excitement and commentary when we reveal our skirts or dresses have real pockets that can actually hold a phone, hankie, Tic Tacs or our Talbot's card.

Lucy Van Pelt told Charlie Brown he was insecure because he

always drew pictures of people with their hands in their pockets. "No," he explained, "I just can't draw hands." Shoving our hands down in our skirt pockets to keep them warm doesn't make us feel insecure, but actually gives us a feeling of power. With pockets, we are organized, focused and ready for action. We aren't weighed down with excess, because our keys, compact, and a little snack are all we need to conquer the world.

Those who graduated from top-tier Southern-charm schools, as well as those who took the discounted online course from Miss Felicity Faith's School of Makeup, Motors and Manners, all know the number-one rule of fashion etiquette; if someone compliments your outfit and it has pockets, you are required to reveal them. It isn't considered bragging, but more of a public service announcement.

"My cousin had pockets sewn into her wedding dress!" said one lady with a sparkly Christmas tree brooch (correctly pinned to her left shoulder). "I've had a dress for 14 years that I refuse to get rid of because it has such great pockets," said an older woman. A cute young mother said her little girl called pockets "cookie holes," and we all agreed she was raising a brilliant child.

There's always one naysayer who points out that adding pockets to clothing makes us look chubby and lumpy. It's the great trade-off of the modern world. Smoothness vs. convenience. Do we want to look svelte and aerodynamic, or do we want a place to put our keys, therefore enabling us to stroll around pocketbook-free? Not having a purse tugging on our arm is liberating. We suddenly feel like Maria von Trapp and are prone to twirl around and sing, with or without a mountaintop.

In addition to our modern gadgets like phones, our pockets can also stash the timeless yet essential basics of a hankie or lipstick — wouldn't it be nice to have our mother's little Avon sample lipsticks from years ago? The perfect small-pocket accessory!

Holiday hostesses need not fret over games like Dirty Santa, Sneaky Santa, Pin the Babe in the Manger, Elf Charades or other reindeer games. All they need for a successful, lively party is a skirt with cookie holes.

A NORMAN ROCKWELL KIND OF MORNING

The year my son started kindergarten, I would set the alarm for 5:45 a.m. and get completely dressed with full makeup and hair done with big hot rollers. I would dress in the outfit I'd carefully chosen the night before, then wake the precious lamb and prepare whole-wheat, made-from-scratch pancakes, shaped like teddy bears, with a sprinkling of blueberries I had picked myself. The syrup came from my great-uncle's cane-grinding the previous Thanksgiving. My darling's lunch box held a dinosaur-shaped sandwich, healthy fruit, homemade cookies from the secret family recipe shaped like the space shuttle (I was big on shaped-theme foods), and of course a note telling him how much Mama loved him. His school clothes were pressed and his red hair sharply parted and slicked down so he looked like Opie. I would walk him to the door of the classroom, kiss him goodbye, and in the afternoons, he would leap into my arms, so happy to see his mommy.

About that time, I remember talking to some women who had high-school children, and they mentioned how terrible their mornings were, with no one able to find anything, the toast burned and everyone banging on the bathroom door. I was relieved my house ran like a well-oiled machine and everyone had their act together for the most perfect of all Norman Rockwell mornings.

Fast forward to third grade. I was able to back up the alarm to around 6:15, because really now, who likes to shower so early? I'd throw on something cute, but sometimes it was what I'd had on the day before, then do my hair — if you consider a ponytail "doing" your hair. Lipstick and mascara was all I had time for before we ran out the door. My son's lunch box contained whatever he had made, since I had grown weary of his not eating my wholesome lunches, so after a friend told me her daughters made their own sandwiches since kindergarten, I got in the groove of teaching "self-sufficiency." The school clothes were clean, but I had discovered spray-on "wrinkle release," so no iron was needed. Thank you to the chemist who invented that! The carpool line was good enough, and as long as I stayed in the car, who would really see what I wore anyway?

By seventh grade, I had two boys to wake, and one of them was a nightmare to get out of bed. By this time, I was setting the alarm 30 minutes later, because I decided all I really needed to do was pull a sweatshirt over my PJs and slap on minimal makeup, that is, if sunglasses and ChapStick are considered makeup. I was coming back home to get fully dressed and fluffed later anyway. Cold cereal was good enough for the boys since we were rushed for time, and lunch was whatever the school cafeteria decided to serve. The boys were growing so fast, they just dug through the laundry and grabbed whatever still fit.

Tenth grade was the last year I had to drive the darlings to school before my eldest was able to take over the chore. I'd roll out of bed when I heard them get up and toss a granola bar their way as they flew out the door. Sometimes they rode the bus with the snarky big kids, because suddenly they were the snarky big kids. I'm not even sure they ate lunch at that point.

Now I only have the youngest son at home and have finally figured out the secret to a smooth morning routine where everyone is relaxed, rested, calm and peaceful . . . we homeschool. The extra sleep is the best medicine in the world for a cranky teenager, and I don't mind it myself. And to all my young friends whose children started school this year with a perfectly cooked breakfast by a perfectly lovely mom, I say . . . just wait. Norman Rockwell mornings have a way of morphing into a crazy, messy — yet somehow beautiful — Picasso.

ICE COLD CONTENTMENT

Early in our marriage, Bob and I had a house that came with a refrigerator that didn't have an ice maker. I know, it was a modern-day, first-world tragedy. It was tough, but after much soul-searching, we decided we had to live with it for a while until we could afford other silly things like food, shelter and baby diapers.

I bought blue plastic ice-cube trays, which weren't easy to find, and I even came across an old metal tray with the pull-lever that was never easy to pull but oh, so quaint and cute. Each cube of ice became a precious commodity in our hot, humid Southern climate. When company came, we'd splurge on store-bought ice and felt like royalty.

One summer, college friends visited, and we didn't have time to get a bag of ice, so we made do with what we had. After dinner, I carefully refilled the trays and put them into the freezer so we'd have lots of ice the next day. But at breakfast, our friend decided to forgo the hot coffee and poured himself a big Co-cola, which is a very Southern way of getting your summer caffeine jolt. Making himself at home, which we loved, he casually dumped an entire tray of ice into his giant tumbler.

Bob and I almost fell over from horror. An entire tray? What would we do for lunch? We've laughed for years about how something as tiny as an ice cube could suddenly become so precious. Our plans for the day immediately changed because one of us had to run to the Gassy-Go and buy more ice.

Focusing on what we don't have reaches beyond material things.

Those who are lonely dream about friends. Those who can't read crave stories. A child without a father only sees daddies everywhere he looks. A broken heart craves love. And yes, there are people in the world who only thirst for clean water, frozen or not. We are wired to focus on what is missing, and to locate the piece of the puzzle that completes us, even when it's something as simple as a cold drink on a humid Alabama day.

After we saved our money and remodeled the kitchen, we splurged and added a separate ice maker. I loved that appliance (almost) more than any child I've had. I'd sit on the floor and polish it until it was as shiny as Miss America's crown. If I put my ear against it, it would hum for me. The magical invention made little nugget-shaped ice with a divot in the center to cuddle our beverages. Sometimes, if we were in a bad mood, we'd extravagantly fill big cups with cubes and swirl them round and round — just to watch them die.

It's only human to want what we don't have and ignore the gifts already present. The tea may be refreshingly sweet, but hey, if it was only cold, we'd love it more.

We moved away from that house and left the ice maker behind. It's true that once a luxury is tasted, it becomes a necessity, because now, even though we have plenty of regular old ice-in-the-door used by most commoners, we still talk about the dreamy olden days when we had a specialized ice maker. Then again, we also reminisce about the simple days when all we needed to make us happy was a case of diapers and a few chunks of ice in our tea.

A BOSTON (FERN) TEA PARTY

Everyone pitches in to help when a small-town church hosts a wedding, and my grandmother's contribution was to loan the bride her massive Boston ferns for decorating the simple sanctuary. Usually, the bride's brothers would arrive at Grandmother's house the day before the wedding to heft the messy plants into the beds of their trucks to carry to the church. The ferns were large enough that multiple trucks were often used so as not to bunch up or break the long fronds. Checking for birds or small animals or even children was a wise use of time, because there's nothing worse than a bird or squirrel getting loose in the church sanctuary the day before your wedding.

Despite being named after the tea party city in the North where they were first discovered, Boston ferns truly love the South and thrive in our humid climate.

Like adding a final swish of lipstick, porches with ferns look pulled together and fully dressed. Grandmother knew the secret to overwintering her ferns in the garage, and when she'd pull them back out in the spring, they were already shooting out bright green growth. Granddaddy would use an axe to divide them, but sadly, like making jelly, I never learned the secret for growing ferns, so year after year, I have to purchase more.

Snatching up the prettiest ferns in town is almost a game, and the phone calls and texts start flying between friends the minute a shipment arrives at the feed and seed or farmer's market. Sometimes the Junior League or marching band will sell them as an easy-as-pie fundraiser because they know everyone in town will need a few.

Assuming you still have a real porch and not a pretend puny slab that some home builders think they can trick us into believing is a porch (shame on them), a fern is one of the must-haves. Rocking chairs and swings are always a plus, and I've written before about how smitten I am with a little lamp by the door that whispers, "Hey! I've been waiting for you to get here!" But if your porch has summertime ferns that spill over like fountains, your house will holler, "Hey, everybody! Nice people live here!"

In past homes, I've had great porches with space for swings, tables, lazy dogs, jumping children and guitar players. Sadly, my current porch would only get an 85 out of 100 on the S.C.S. (Southern Charm Scale). It's a tight fit, but we've squeezed a few rocking chairs in there, although they are arranged like a jailhouse lineup, which actually makes some family members feel quite at home (married into the family, not blood kin). It gets a few extra-credit points for being close enough to a pasture where we can hear mooing cows on one side and laughter from children on the other, but no matter what I try to do to make it comfortable, it never feels quite right until I get the ferns out there in the spring.

The variegated greenery provides a stunning backdrop for the romantic bride, dressed in white. The perfect trifecta of a Southern wedding is billowing ferns, winding ivy, and waxy magnolia leaves. Live plants bring the warmth of home into the formal service and represent eternal -evergreen love. Wandie

Leslie Anne Tarabella

Fisher from Waycross didn't have access to any real ferns, so she taped some artificial Christmas tree branches to the pews. It was the talk of the county for an entire decade.

Ferns on the porch pull us away from our indoor blinking gadgets and force us to sweep up their fluff, which in turn leads us to linger awhile, wave to dog-walking neighbors, listen to the birds and sit a spell to drink a glass of icy tea. It's the plant that inspires us to have our own version of a Boston (fern) tea party.

COLORFUL KITCHEN MEMORIES

We can thank the "color-ologists" at Pantone for giving us a new reason to look forward to January. At the beginning of every year, they announce their official "Color of the Year." It's a very big deal for decorators and designers and, much to my husband's fear, always makes me contemplate repainting a room or two.

The color experts provide deep psychological reasons for their choice, and it always has something to do with making us feel peaceful, safe, happy and loved. For Southerners, our minds will naturally wind their way back to the colors of a kitchen we've loved.

Food is an important part of our culture, so our memories of living rooms, bedrooms and patios can fade, but even if it's been several decades since we were last there, we can still identify the exact pattern and shade of the curtains, dishes, countertops and walls of a kitchen where we were warm, well fed and safe.

People may first remember how ugly the harvest gold appliances were. Soon, however, they'll come around to telling you about how they loved sitting at the mid-century atomic-patterned

Formica counter while Granny made biscuits and pulled turquoise Fiesta Ware out of the canary-yellow cabinets.

My sorority sister Verbie Jo laughs about her great-aunt's pink kitchen with poodle dish towels, yet every time she passes through an antique store, she searches for pink Pyrex for her own collection.

Our food is legendary, and the kitchens where it was prepared hold memories more colorful and detailed than any company-issued paint swatch. This year's passing trend will soon be forgotten, yet the color of our great-granny's kitchen step stool we stood on to help stir the stew will stick with us until we die.

My favorite color has been orange for a long while now (maybe because of *The Brady Bunch* kitchen?), but my love of green probably started in my grandmother's kitchen. With innovative flip-out cabinet space to hold dry goods, the kitchen had floors with a Kelly green and white checkerboard pattern. When I see a similar floor now, I instantly break into a smile and crave tea cakes, which were always in a cookie jar on the counter.

Smelling the warm aroma of a yellow butter cake, licking a chocolate-coated spoon shiny clean, and spotting a silver pot bubbling with eggs yet to be deviled: all came from Grandmother's green kitchen. It was small, yet somehow held her along with four daughters, reaching, flipping, chopping food and shooing children out of the way.

Linoleum patterns, chair cushions and tablecloths edged in hand-embroidered daisies are seared into our minds and produce far more of a psychological response of peace, safety and happiness than any commercial paint swatch chosen for us (by a company based in New Jersey, by the way — "Not that there's anything wrong with that," said my NJ husband).

Not only the heart of the home, the kitchen is a place that is held deep within our real hearts. Our memories of colors, smells, tastes and sounds can be as sharp as if we were just sitting there yesterday.

Pantone feeds our need for something new, but we only need to close our eyes to be nourished in the colors and patterns of a kitchen we've loved, even if it's harvest gold, orange or pink poodle paradise.

MAKING IT EASIER TO LET GO

Older women would see my children and say, "Enjoy them while they're young. They grow up in a hurry." I'd smile and think, "That's sweet," but what I didn't understand was they were actually revealing the secret for not losing my mind years later when my children walked out the door into the world. The ultimate secret for having a happy transition to an empty nest isn't anything you can do the last few months before they leave, but instead, it's something you have to work on during the previous 18 years.

These women knew the secret to successfully launching teenagers into the world is connected to what you do when they're much younger.

Imagine that, those older women really were wiser.

If they had been more specific, these ladies would have explained that when we walk away and leave them sitting in the dorm or put them on the bus for basic training, it won't be as gut-wrenching if we've really and truly enjoyed our time with them. Not so much repetitive sporting events or dance recitals, but real, honest-to-goodness time spent with silly, crying, foot-stomping, hugging and giggling children.

The first few times you choke up as you set the table with one less plate, you won't think of the expensive vacations you took. Instead, you'll smile at the memory of them hiding their lima beans under their plates or spilling milk or telling knock-knock jokes while slurping spaghetti.

The small quick moments of parenting meld together and form a fortress of strength for the breaking heart of a lonely parent. The memory of a dirty-faced little boy falling asleep in your arms with his stinky little head on your chest is the perfect antidote for not having anyone to tuck in at night.

Taking time away from your desk, phone and computer to spend time with your children is like stocking up the pantry before a hurricane. When others are starving for just a little more time and crying for one more memory or one more experience, you'll be satisfied with bountiful plenty because you've enjoyed them. You've delighted in their achievements and secretly smiled at their mistakes, because you know (hope) it's how they learn.

When your son calls to say he's taking a girl to a dance, you'll be comforted by the memory of being his first dance partner, twirling around the kitchen to the dreamy smell of chicken potpie. When your daughter tells you she's pledged a sorority and they had the fanciest party in the world, you'll know she secretly compared it to the princess party you threw for her eighth birthday.

Parents of young children don't realize that when they fall into bed exhausted every single night after chasing naked children around the house, begging them to put on their pajamas before they freeze to death, they are really making it easier to let go in a few years. A storybook here, a broken lamp there, bouncing on the bed and Eskimo kisses will ultimately help you send them on their way.

The older moms were trying to tell me it's all about making memories and not taking a moment for granted. Trading a few business meetings for marshmallow roasts or tee times for teddy bear picnics will leave both you and your teen fulfilled and regret free. Enjoy them while they're young, because graduation is closer than you think.

SUNDAY SCHOOL ARTS AND CRAFTS

My favorite thing about going to church when I was a little girl was arts and crafts time. I loved making things and spent more time creating paper plate tambourines and Bible verse paper chains than any other kid in town. I could literally write a book about how to use toilet paper rolls to create a tribute to every single book of the Bible, all the animals in the ark, and if glitter was added, the resurrection itself.

When I was old enough to start GAs, or the Baptist version of Girl Scouts, I was thrilled to learn we'd be making banks. We planned to use them to collect our spare change, then in a month or so, after dinner in the fellowship hall, we'd box it all up and send it to the missionaries. All the other girls began to brainstorm how they'd collect the most money, but all I cared about was having the most spectacular-looking bank.

I found an empty Nestlé's Quick canister at home and managed to cut a slit in the round metal lid. In those days, no one worried or cared that I probably used Daddy's tools and could have easily sliced my hand off. Next, I covered the can in beautiful sky-blue construction paper, then made an overall collage with photos I'd cut out of my mother's WMU book of missionaries reading to half-naked children.

I guess the photos of the naked children finally touched my wee heart, because I decided I needed to earn extra money, so I went to my neighbors' houses and hit them up for spare nickels and dimes.

Just before I left on my fundraising quest, I realized my hamster hadn't been on a field trip in a long time. It therefore made sense to put Bubbles inside the bank, keeping the lid loose, so he could breathe. When change was plunked into the bank, Bubbles made a little game out of dodging the coins. However, when I came to Mrs. Adams's house, she insisted on giving me a dollar bill. Before I could stop her, she reached down and lifted the metal lid, and of course, Bubbles popped his head out to say hello.

You would have thought Jesus himself had popped out of that canister with all the yodeling and hollering that went on. Bubbles survived, but I think Mrs. Adams still owes me that dollar.

As I grew older and arts and crafts were phased out, I realized my love of church crafts didn't stem from the artwork itself. What I truly enjoyed was the closeness we spent while sitting around the little tables and talking to each other. We weren't having a formal lesson about Moses, but instead, our Sunday School teachers were listening to our childhood worries, silliness and concerns.

As we used tissue paper to make stained-glass windows, Mike told us about his dog dying and we all decided Rufus was in heaven. Our sweet teachers used gentle voices and told us how they liked the way we shared with each other, then asked Pamela how her grandmother was feeling. The teachers said they'd pray for our families and upcoming math tests. They bragged on the way we invited new friends to sit with us. While I colored the Red Sea red, I told everyone about my baby brother, and my teacher said babies were precious gifts from God. We encouraged and marveled at our friend Rose, who didn't have a mother at home and told us how she made her own breakfast, and our teacher told her God loved her very much.

Whenever I've worked with children, I've tried to remember to provide plenty of time for arts and crafts, because there just may be a little girl who seems like she's making a diorama of the Holy Land (that could double as her hamster's habitat), but she simply needs someone to sit and talk to her. Providing children with glue, scissors, kindness, encouragement and love can result in the most beautiful masterpiece of all.

WHEN A SOUTHERN LADY WALKS INTO A ROOM

She walked into the room, impeccably dressed in a blue and white patterned top with matching navy skirt. Her jewelry sparkled and her hair was perfect. Her bright smile was greater than the Mona Lisa's yet less than Miss America's. Her final yet essential accessory was the hint of mischief in her eyes, which instantly drew everyone in the room to her. My 101-year-old friend Jule Moon is the best example of a Southern lady I've ever seen.

It doesn't matter how old they are, Southern women know how to enter a room, sit down, not say a word, and still be the center of attention. They don't do it on purpose, because truth be told, they were taught to shun the spotlight. Like their heartbeat, it's just something that happens naturally, without plan or thought.

Generations of little girls have watched closely as their mothers, aunts and grannies smoothed their hair, pinched their cheeks and straightened their dresses just before they entered a room. They've learned through observation that standing up straight and not slouching means you have respect for the people around you. Good conversation and looking someone in the eye when they speak lets them know you value what they say. As teens, they were told, "Put on some lipstick and stop that whining!" This sent the message that their drama was not appropriate outside of the home.

Ladies like Jule have mastered the art of making others feel special and appreciated, which is the basis for all good Southern manners.

Business meetings, social committees and church services have all come to a halt when a great Southern lady has shown up. Age doesn't matter, but usually the more seasoned ones like Jule have perfected the art and can wow a crowd with far less effort than those much younger. I've watched as a simple nod of the head, smile or eye contact from a lady have made the speaker lose their concentration, while others jump to their feet to offer a choice seat.

Born in Atlanta and raised by loving parents and a mother who was friendly with Margaret Mitchell, Jule moved to Mobile when she was 12 years old and eventually attended Murphy High School, where she was involved in many activities and served as the editor of the school newspaper. She later graduated from the University of Texas and worked in many different careers, including counseling and geology. She dabbled in real estate and became a prolific writer, and like many Southerners who value history and a good story, she has a passion for antiques.

Gliding, sashaying or floating into a room, never tromping, stomping or slinking, Jule sometimes carries a cane; yet in her hands, it seems more like a magic wand than walking aid, proving she knows the Southern secret of transforming anything into an elegant accessory.

Chic enough to appreciate designer frocks, Jule is confident and savvy enough to find the best styles at the thrift shop. She once discovered a sparkling evening gown at Goodwill and wore it to claim the title of "Best Dressed" in the Mrs. Senior Baldwin Pageant.

Some women are wrecks, others cause them. Some scream for attention, while others quietly grab it with a grin. Time comes to a standstill, so age means nothing when a great Southern lady walks into the room.

AUTHOR'S NOTE

A Southerner always has a difficult time saying goodbye, so for now I'll say, "so long" and thank you for reading. I find inspiration in the notes and letters I receive from you and think your stories could fill thousands of books. You can stay in touch by following me on AL.com or on my blog, leslieannetarabella.com.

Until we meet again at the beginning of a really great story that begins, "come over here and sit down, I've got something good to tell you!" I wish you all the blessings and joy in this world.

Leslie Anne

CPSIA information can be obtained
at www.ICGtesting.com
Printed in the USA
LVHW051111291020
670168LV00002B/254

9 781664 206533